Presented by

Smart
People
Should
Build
Things

ANDREW YANG

Smart People Should Build Things

How to Restore Our Culture of Achievement, Build a Path for Entrepreneurs, and Create New Jobs in America

HARPER
BUSINESS

An Imprint of HarperCollins*Publishers*
www.harpercollins.com

HarperCollins books may be purchased for educational, business, or sales promotional use. For information, please e-mail the Special Markets Department at SPsales@harpercollins.com.

FIRST EDITION

Designed by Jo Anne Metsch

Library of Congress Cataloging-in-Publication Data has been applied for.

ISBN: 978-0-06-229204-9

14 15 16 17 18 OV/RRD 10 9 8 7 6 5 4 3 2 1

*This book is dedicated to everyone who helped bring
Venture for America into the world and continues
to support our organization's progress.
We're grateful each day.*

Contents

Contents

Introduction

We've got a problem: our smart people are doing the wrong things. If we can get them to do the right things, it will transform the country.

It was 2000, and Charlie Kroll was a senior about to graduate from Brown University. He had his heart set on returning to New York City and becoming an investment banker; he studied economics and was the treasurer of the Brown Investment Group. To his surprise, he didn't get the position he wanted with Morgan Stanley, despite being a strong student who had interned at Morgan Stanley and UBS in New York and London the previous two summers. He recovered from his disappointment quickly, and started a website development company, Andera, out of his dorm room. He submitted his business plan to a college competition, and though he didn't win, his adviser saw a spark in Charlie and offered to invest some seed money. Over the following year, Charlie was able to raise $300,000, and his company grew from one to six employees. Things looked promising.

Then, in 2001, the tech bubble burst. No one wanted to

pay top dollar for a website. Andera struggled, even threatening to miss payroll a few times, with Charlie worrying what he'd say to his employees as he let them go. At one point, he even asked his girlfriend Jen to invest, which she did. She must have had real faith in him, because Charlie wasn't sure where his company was headed at the time.

Charlie fought to keep Andera afloat. During his third year in business, he met with the head of a regional bank and pitched Andera's website services to her. After he gave his pitch, she said, "Thanks for the presentation, but let me tell you what I'm really interested in. We need something that would help our customers open accounts online more easily. Is that something you could help with?"

"Sure," Charlie said. "We can do that." He then went back to his office to figure out just what would be involved in solving the bank executive's problem. A few months later, his company had a new customer and a new direction. Andera found its niche helping regional banks provide some of the same online convenience as the big national banks. It gained dozens—and then hundreds—of community banks as customers. Jen's investment paid off in more ways than one; the couple got married a few years later and now they have two beautiful children. Today, Andera is a multimillion-dollar software company employing almost a hundred people in Providence, Rhode Island, a city that has an unemployment rate of over 10 percent.

If Morgan Stanley had offered Charlie that job, Andera probably wouldn't exist, Providence's unemployment rate would be a little bit higher, and regional banks would be a little bit less competitive. But what if Charlie were the norm instead of the exception? What if the same level of talent that is currently heading to finance or law school or management consulting instead went to starting or developing growth companies like Andera? What if 25 percent of our top graduates went to startups around the country each year instead of to Wall Street? How long would that take to generate thousands of new jobs, companies, opportunities, and even industries?

This book is going to help answer these questions.

I believe there's a basic solution to our country's economic and social problems. We need to get our smart people building things (again). They're not really doing it right now. They'd like to. But they're being led down certain paths during and after college and told not to worry, they can figure it out later.

Take me, for instance. I wasn't nearly as enterprising as Charlie when I graduated from Brown in 1996. I had a general desire to be smart, accomplished, and successful— whatever that meant. So I went to law school and became a corporate attorney in New York.

I figured out I was in the wrong place after a number of months working at the law firm. I left in less than a year and cofounded a dot-com company, Stargiving, which helped raise money for celebrity-affiliated nonprofits. It was extraordinarily difficult. My company failed spectacularly, but I recovered. I went to work for a mobile software company, Crisp Wireless, and then a health care software company, MMF Systems, over the next five years, eventually becoming the CEO of a test-prep company, Manhattan GMAT, in 2006.

I spent five years running Manhattan GMAT, helping young people get into business school. I taught our corporate classes of investment banking analysts and consultants at Goldman Sachs, McKinsey and Company, JPMorgan Chase,

Morgan Stanley, and Deloitte, as well as hundreds of individual students over the years. Some were exactly where they wanted to be. But there seemed to be just as many top-notch young people who wondered why they didn't like their jobs more. They sought a higher sense of engagement with their work and their careers. Sometimes they would put words to what they were looking for; they'd say they wanted "something entrepreneurial" or "to be really excited about something."

By the time my company was acquired by Kaplan and its parent, the Washington Post Company, in 2009, I knew a few things. I knew that there were promising startups and growth companies all over the country that needed talent to expand and thrive. I knew firsthand that there was an army of talented, ambitious, somewhat directionless young people who'd love to work for a startup. And I knew that if we could connect these two groups, we'd help everyone: the individuals, the companies, cities and communities around the country, the economy, and society as a whole.

When I was younger, I subscribed to a general view of our educational system that goes something like this: If you study hard and do well in high school, you'll get into a good college. Where you go to college is very important. Then, if you do well in college, perhaps you'll go on to law school or med school, or maybe academia if you're an intellectual sort. In any case, if you're smart and work hard, you'll wind up with a good job.

That "good job," in this scenario, is a job that requires a lot of complex analytical thinking and pays well, like investment banking or management consulting. If a student takes a professional route, becoming a lawyer, doctor, accountant, or dentist, he or she will need additional years of special training to develop professional skills and judgment—all very attractive to high achievers.

This is our system of training and employment, and it functions very well. Smart, hardworking kids go to good schools and get trained for good jobs. The job market operates with great efficiency, and that is a big reason why our economy is so successful.

There's another view of the current system, though—that it's a mess. Ambitious college students have no real idea what to do upon graduation, but they're trained to seek the "next level." Many apply to law school, grad school, or even medical school because of a vague notion of status and progress rather than a genuine desire or natural fit. Those who try to do something independently often find themselves frustrated by their lack of rapid advancement, and so default to a more structured path of law school, business school, or graduate school. The concentration in professional services leads our national university graduates to congregate in a handful of metropolitan areas—primarily New York City, Silicon Valley, Boston, and Washington, DC. Those who become bankers or consultants are highly paid and heavily socialized, yet many become disaffected due to a lack of purpose or unsustainable lifestyle, and some simply discover they don't enjoy their roles. We train thousands more lawyers each year than legal jobs exist for, and hundreds more academics than there are academic jobs. Each path throws off waves of refugees who are often at a loss as to what to do with themselves, only at that point they're in their late twenties, possibly in debt or used to an expensive lifestyle, and trained to do something narrow and specific.

Meanwhile, massive needs in other sectors are not being met. American companies need smart people who can manage, operate, innovate, and improve them. And startups and early-stage growth companies are in desperate need of talent in order to create jobs and drive economic progress. The metropolitan areas of Detroit, New Orleans, Baltimore, Philadelphia, Cleveland, Cincinnati, and Las Vegas account for over $1 trillion of US gross domestic product and represent a vastly diverse range of industries. The trajectory of the young growth companies in these cities and others like them will determine the direction of our economy. Detroit alone is our twelfth largest metro region, with over 3.6 million people. Its post-bankruptcy renewal is one of the great projects of this age. Unfortunately, it doesn't have a giant recruitment arm to make the case on college campuses.

Our identification and distribution of talent in the United States has gone from being a historic strength to a critical weakness. We've let the market dictate what our smart kids do, and they're being systematically funneled into obvious, structured paths that don't serve them or the economy terribly well.

This book makes a basic argument. If year after year we send our top people to financial services, management consulting, and law schools, we'll wind up with the pattern we're already seeing: layers of highly paid professionals working astride faltering companies and industries. But if we send them to startups, we'll get something else. Early-stage companies in energy, retail, biotech, consumer products, health care, transportation, software, media, education, and other industries would have a better chance of innovating and creating value. Even allowing for a certain amount of failure, we'd create hundreds of new companies and tens of thousands of new jobs over time. Our economy and our country would be better off. Our communities' tax bases would go up, shoring up our ability to pay for schools and long-term development. We'd restore our culture of achievement to include value creation, risk and reward, and the common good. By solving this one problem, we solve many other problems at the same time.

The first part of this book details our current system of allocating talent, where our top graduates go, what they're doing, and why it's not leading where we'd like to go. As you'll see, it's entirely predictable that if someone attends a national university, the odds of him or her doing certain things skyrocket and the odds of choosing other pursuits correspondingly plummet. We are hyperallocating the bulk of our top graduates to professional services industries—finance, consulting, and law—and concentrating that talent in cities like New York, San Francisco, Boston, Chicago, Los Angeles, and Washington, DC, while leaving promising new companies around the country underresourced. In 1982, companies that had been in business less than five years made up almost half of all American companies. By 2011, that number had declined to slightly more than a third. Over that same period, the percentage of America's workforce employed by new companies dropped from over 20 percent to less than 11 percent, and in 2008, for the first time, the majority of U.S. workers worked at companies with 500 or more employees.[1]

New firms are responsible for most of the job growth and innovation in our economy. A Kauffman Foundation study showed that new firms accounted for all net job growth in the United States from 1977 to 2005.[2] In the United States, firms with fewer than 500 employees account for thirteen times more patents per employee than larger firms.[3] If you want to spur long-term job growth, you want as much talent as possible heading to new firms so that more of those firms can succeed, expand, and hire even more people. Having the right people early on can make the difference between success and failure. Yet these companies are often unable to recruit the people they need from day one. When policy makers talk about startups, they always seem to fixate on access to capital and investor incentives. Meanwhile, if you talk to entrepreneurs, they will tell you that access to human and intellectual capital is the key ingredient that's often missing. They know that human capital attracts financial capital, as well as the reverse. Money follows talent. Imagine if every promising growth company in the country had a nucleus of top prospects waiting to join it every year; how long would this take to impact job growth and innovation?

This problem can be solved. I run Venture for America, a nonprofit organization that recruits dozens of our country's top graduates each year and places them in startups and growth companies in Detroit, New Orleans, Las Vegas, Providence, Cincinnati, Baltimore, Cleveland, Philadelphia, and other cities around the country. Our goal is to help create 100,000 new US jobs by 2025. We supply talent to early-stage companies so that they can expand and hire more people. And we train a critical mass of our best and brightest graduates to build enterprises and create new opportunities for themselves and others.

The best way to become an entrepreneur is to learn from a more experienced leader as he or she builds a company. We provide that operating experience, as well as training, networks, and support for enterprising college graduates who are accepted into our two-year program. We also offer seed funding to some of the Venture Fellows who perform well and want to start their own businesses. Our goal is to make it as straightforward to become a startup manager or entrepreneur in Detroit or New Orleans as it currently is to be a professional in New York City or Washington, DC.

But our efforts remain only one piece of the puzzle. It's my hope that after reading this book, you'll understand how the pieces fit together, and perhaps we'll all be able to see what can happen when we affect the most important determinant of our shared future—where our talent is going— and do something about it.

A couple of notes on terminology—particularly this book's title, *Smart People Should Build Things*. We're using educational attainment as an imperfect proxy for "smart" and talking about people who get tracked, sorted, and aggregated throughout their adolescence into various universities and courses of study. For example, Shilpi Kumar is a recent graduate of Duke University with a degree in neuroscience. This book will oversimplify matters by focusing on people like Shilpi who get identified as "smart" or "talented" via our national educational system. It's clear that there are different forms of intelligence (analytical, creative, linguistic, artistic, interpersonal, athletic/kinesthetic, and so on), and that not all brilliant and talented people go to college or even graduate from high school. But for structural and practical reasons, this book will focus on those who do.

By "building things," we mean forming and helping companies and organizations that are innovating and creating value. People and companies around the country are solving real problems right now. For example, in New Orleans, Venture for America works with a company called Kickboard that provides a software application to help teachers track student performance. Kickboard was founded by Jen Medbery, who studied computer science at Columbia University and taught middle-schoolers through Teach for America. Jen created the product that she wished she'd had as a teacher. Now she's building a company; Kickboard has dozens of school districts as clients and has grown to more than twelve employees.

ShapeUp is a health care tech company in Providence that helps individuals promote health and wellness through social networking and goal measurement. It was founded by two Brown University MDs, Dr. Rajiv Kumar and Dr. Brad Weinberg, who noticed that patients who successfully changed their lifestyles and lost weight benefited immensely when they received encouragement from friends, family, and colleagues. Companies pay ShapeUp because fitter employees save employers money through reduced health care costs, increased productivity, and decreased absenteeism. Rajiv and Brad saw a way to both improve human health and build a growth business. Venture for America sent ShapeUp its newest web designer, Johnny Hung.

Accio Energy is a clean tech company in Ann Arbor, Michigan, that is designing a next-generation wind-electric power generator with no moving blades. Accio's design utilizes the interaction of air and water, simulating phenomena that occur naturally during thunderstorms. Its office includes a warehouse with a wind tunnel to test upgrades. Accio's CEO, Jennifer Baird, previously cofounded and sold another startup for $205 million, and Accio's president and chief technology officer, Dawn White, has a PhD in mechanical engineering and twenty patents to her name. The company's Venture for America Fellow is Tim Dingman, an electrical engineer who helps Accio with their design simulations.

Just minutes away from Accio in Detroit you'll find Are You a Human, a software company that is replacing those annoying website Captchas (you know, the ones where you're forced to retype illegible and often nonsensical words) with miniature branded games, like launching a hockey puck through the goal. It was founded by two University of Michigan entrepreneurs, Reid Tatoris and Tyler Paxton, and funded by Detroit Venture Partners. Max Nussenbaum, an English major from Wesleyan University, is the Venture Fellow helping get the word out about their product.[*]

Charlie, Jen, Rajiv, Brad, Jennifer, Dawn, Reid, and Tyler are examples of smart people building things. Chances are, this is the first you're hearing about them or their companies. Talented people like them are doing great work and solving problems around the country, but not as many as we need. This book is meant to change that.

---

[*]Not every problem or company involves high technology. Kristin Groos Richmond and Kirsten Tobey saw that not enough kids were getting healthy, affordable meals in public schools. They started Revolution Foods in 2006 to provide healthy meals to schoolchildren at a competitive price. Today, Revolution Foods prepares almost 200,000 meals a day for over six hundred schools in nine states and has nearly a thousand community-hired employees.

PART ONE

Where Our Talent Is Going

1

The Prestige Pathways

If you graduate from a national university, there's a very good chance that you're going to become a banker, lawyer, consultant, or doctor, and the odds are high that you're going to pursue one of these professions in New York, Boston, San Francisco, Los Angeles, Chicago, or Washington, DC, regardless of where you originally grew up.

Why is that?

It's because achievers want to achieve, and that's what achievement now looks like.

I'm an example. I was not a particularly motivated or passionate young person, unless you consider playing lots of Dungeons and Dragons in the suburbs of New York City to be a cue for future entrepreneurship. As a kid, my parents told me that my job was to get into a good college, which involved getting good grades, playing piano at a competitive level, and playing tennis well enough to make my mediocre high school team.

When I was twelve, they started sending me to an academic summer camp run by Johns Hopkins University.

"Nerd camp," we called it, though its official name was the Center for (Academically) Talented Youth (CTY). I took the SAT as a preteen to qualify. I loved CTY—it was the home of my awkward first kiss and my first girlfriend, where weeks seemed to last for entire seasons.

When I was fourteen, one of my summer camp mates, Lucy, mentioned that she went to a prep school in New England called Exeter and liked it. I pitched going there to my parents. I was kind of coasting at my public school, half-heartedly doing well enough to maintain my general profile as the smart kid but not really pushing too hard.

My parents were thrilled with the idea, and I headed off to Phillips Exeter Academy when I was fifteen. It was a phenomenal place to get an education; I appreciate it a great deal now that I've had time to reflect on all that I gained from my time there. But it's not an easy environment. As one example, postgraduates were recruited to play every major sport at the school to make the teams supercompetitive, so a lot of young people were forced to reassess their identities because they could no longer make a team. In my teenage mind, going to Exeter was largely about getting into college. My most significant extracurricular activity was being a member of the debate team. I performed well at a New England prep school debate and was named to the US national team. We went to the world championships in London, where I promptly got blown out of the water by anyone with a British accent.

I got into Stanford and Brown, and after visiting both schools, decided to go to Brown. Stanford seemed way too nice and pleasant in terms of climate and architecture—I had a hard time imagining myself or anyone working particularly hard there, probably because I'd been conditioned by harsh northeastern winters. Also, my family lived on the East Coast, and it was appealing to be close to them. I showed up at Brown planning on getting a degree in English, but after a semester of reading *Moll Flanders* I switched to economics and political science.

My parents did a great job of conditioning my brother and me to be conscious of money. I was on a partial scholarship to Brown that was provided by IBM, but I felt the pressure. My parents were always doing things like sucking marrow out of bones and eating fish heads, and reminding me how they'd mortgaged the house to cover my tuition. I got an on-campus job as a snack bar worker making six dollars per hour and was promoted to supervisor after a semester. I'd worked part-time at the library while at Exeter, and thus took for granted that I should have a job all of the time.

My spare time at Brown was spent working out, training at tae kwon do (I maxed out below the black belt level; I wasn't terribly good at it), and playing video games. On the way to one tae kwon do competition at Cornell, my cologne spilled onto my uniform (why pack cologne for a martial arts tournament?), and I walked around reeking of Claiborne for Men all weekend. My teammates noticed, and started saying things like, "He smells too sexy to hit!" Unfortunately, my opponents disagreed.

Probably my proudest achievement in college was that I could bench-press 225 pounds eight times in a row. I named my pectorals Lex and Rex, and could jostle them on command to make them "talk." I was also one of a handful of top *Street Fighter II* players on campus, and could even compete credibly with Balrog and other marginal characters.

If the above description makes me sound like a fairly

unremarkable student at Brown, that's about right. I did well in my economics courses but didn't excel in any serious-minded way. I spent my summers returning to CTY as a resident adviser, which was a fun job. I also worked as a busboy at a Chinese restaurant in Westchester County, New York, for a couple of summers, but my written Chinese was too cruddy to translate orders to the chefs, and the fact that I spoke English well really confused the patrons. At the end of the night, all of the other workers would get into a minibus and head to New York City's Chinatown while I got into my parents' Honda Accord and drove home.

Around junior year, I began thinking about going to law school. It wasn't a terribly sophisticated process. Thanks to my family's emphasis on education, I always assumed I'd go on to some kind of additional schooling. I wanted to become a smart, successful guy, and law school seemed like a good way to go. I took the LSAT and got a 178, which further made it seem like the thing to do. The end of my undergraduate career was uneventful. I took my senior spring courses on a pass/fail basis, and spent most of my senior year moping about my ex-girlfriend, who'd left me while I had studied abroad in Hong Kong the previous year.

I headed off to Columbia Law School a few months after graduation. I took out student loans to pay for it—about $40,000 per year. I kept my head down and tried to do well. I wound up on the *Law Review*, and got offered jobs by each of the top firms in New York as a second-year student. I took a job at Davis Polk and Wardwell after graduating because it seemed to have more of a humanist environment than the others, and I started working in the banking and mergers and acquisitions departments. I was twenty-four years old, making $125,000 a year plus an annual bonus of about $15,000. I owed $110,000 in law school debt, despite working both summers and part-time during my third year of law school being overpaid by the firm to perform research tasks.

As you can see, there's not much to indicate anything unconventional up to this point. It wasn't until I got to the law firm that things started hitting me. First, the people around me seemed pretty unhappy. You can go to any corporate law firm and see dozens of people whose satisfaction with their jobs is below average.

The work was entirely uninspiring. We were for the most part grease on a wheel, helping shepherd transactions along; it was detail-intensive and often quite dull. Only years later did I realize what our economic purpose was: if a transaction was large enough, you had to pay a team of people to pore over documents into the wee hours to make sure nothing went wrong.

I had zero attachment to my clients—not unusual, given that I was the last rung down on the ladder, and most of the time I only had a faint idea of who my clients were. Someone above me at the firm would give me a task, and I'd do it.

I also kind of thought that being a corporate lawyer would help me with the ladies. Not so much, just so you know.

It was true that I was getting paid a lot for a twenty-four-year-old with almost no experience. I made more than my father, who has a PhD in physics and had generated dozens of patents for IBM over the years. It seemed kind of ridiculous to me; what the heck had I done to deserve that kind of money? As you can tell, not a whole lot. That didn't keep my colleagues from pitching a fit if the lawyers across the street were making one dollar more than we were.

Most worrisome of all, my brain started to rewire itself after only the first few months. I was adapting. I started spotting issues in offering memoranda. My ten-thousand-yard unblinking document review stare got better and better. Holy cow, I thought—if I don't leave soon, I'm going to become good at this and wind up doing it for a long time.

My experience is a tiny data point in a much bigger problem.

Let's imagine a very large company. It is a leader in its industry and much admired by its peers. It invests a tremendous amount of money—literally billions of dollars a year—in identifying, screening, and training its many employees. Those employees who are considered to have high potential are sent to special training programs at substantial additional cost. Happily, these top training programs are considered to be among the best in the world.

After these employees complete their training, the company encourages them to choose for themselves the division in which they'd like to work. Employee preferences are deemed to be the most efficient way of deciding who works where. This seems like a good system, and it works well for a long time. However, perhaps predictably, many of its most highly rated employees eventually become drawn to the finance and legal divisions because these divisions have very effective recruitment arms, are more visible, pay better, and are thought of as providing a more intellectual level of work. Over time, proportionally fewer of the top recruits go toward the management of the company or the company's operations. The company's basic training division is considered a backwater, with low pay and low recognition. And only a relative handful of employees go toward research and development or the launching of any new products.

Take a second to think about the company described above. What do you think will happen to this company as time passes? And if you think that it's not set on a path to success, what would you do to fix it? This company reflects, in essence, the economy of the United States of America.

If you are a smart college student and you want to become a lawyer and go to law school, what you must do has been well established. You must go to a good school, get good grades (already accomplished, for many), and take the LSAT (a four-hour skill test). There is no anxiety in divining the requirements, as they are clearly spelled out. Most undergrads, even those with little interest in law school, know what it takes to get in. The *path location costs* are low.

The same is true if you want to become a doctor. Becoming a doctor is hard, right? Sort of. It is arduous and time-consuming, but it is not hard if you have certain academic abilities. You must take a battery of college courses (organic chemistry being the most infamous and rigorous of them) and do well, study for the MCAT (an eight-hour exam), and spend a summer or even a year caddying for a researcher, doctor, or hospital. These are time-consuming hoop-jumping tasks, to be sure, but anyone with a very high level of academic aptitude can complete them.

If you attend an Ivy League university or similar national institution, legions of suit-wearing representatives from the big-name investment banks and consulting firms will show up at your campus and conduct first-round interviews to fill their ranks each year, even in a down period (as with the recent years following the financial crisis). They will spend millions of dollars enlisting interns and educating the market annually. Most freshmen have no idea what management consulting is, yet seniors can rattle off the distinctions of different firms with little difficulty. All undergraduates have friends in the classes above them who have gone through this process and gained analyst or associate positions at major investment banks and consulting firms. Again, the requirements are clear: you have to have good grades, be able to perform some cognitive tasks with words and numbers in the form of case studies that you should prepare for and practice, and hopefully look good in a suit. It is also very helpful if you spend a summer in college doing something that can be presented as relating to your professional interest; in many cases it's necessary that you intern at the employer the summer before your senior year in order to get an offer. Summer internships have become vital for getting jobs in the most selective firms, so the process begins quite early—junior year at the latest. This path requires some early choices, but you don't have to spend time taking another standardized test. Of course, many of the people who go into finance and consulting take the GMAT and go on to business school.

These structured paths are clearly laid out, and are pursued collectively by many—or most—of the students who have been screened and sorted as the academic and cognitive elite. These "prestige pathways" have become the default options. In 2011, 29 percent of employed Harvard graduates went into finance or consulting, while 19 percent of the class applied to law school and 18 percent applied to medical school.[1] That's a majority of the class. California (San Francisco), New York (New York City), and Massachusetts

(Boston) were the only states that received over one hundred Harvard grads in 2012, with Illinois (Chicago) and Washington, DC, being the only other destinations to receive fifty or more.[2] The statistics from Yale, Dartmouth, Penn, and other top schools are similar.

Perhaps this is somewhat surprising—wouldn't college students at these top schools be positioned to blaze their own trails and pursue less conventional routes with the access that they have been given?

Unfortunately, hardworking, academically gifted young people are kind of lazy when it comes to determining direction. If you give them a hoop to jump through, jumping through that hoop can take two, twenty, or two hundred hours, and it won't make a big difference. But they are quite lazy when it comes to figuring out what path to take or—more profoundly—building their own path. They're trained to get the grade or ace the application. That is what has made them successful in most every conventional respect each step of the way up to their senior year in college, at the point that this process is well under way.

"It's doing a process that you've done a billion times before," explains Dylan Matthews, a 2012 Harvard graduate who wrote for the campus newspaper, the *Harvard Crimson*, before becoming a journalist. He adds,

> Everyone who goes to Harvard went hard on the college application process. Applying to Wall Street is much closer to that than applying anywhere else is. There are a handful of firms you really care about, they all have formal application processes that they walk you through, there's a season when it all happens, all of them come to you and interview

11

you where you live. Harvard students are really good at formal processes like that, and they're less good at going on Monster or Craigslist and sorting through thousands of job listings from thousands of companies whose reputations they don't know. Wall Street and consulting (and Teach for America, too) turn applying to jobs into applying to college [again], more or less.[3]

Of course, the same procedural comfort level applies to law school and other graduate programs, and the same mindset pervades competitive campuses around the country.

You could ask, so what if our talented young people all march off to become lawyers, doctors, bankers, and consultants? Isn't that what smart people are *supposed* to do?

There are a few problems with this stance. First, the degree to which the recruitment infrastructure exists is a relatively recent phenomenon. Bain and Company, a premier management-consulting firm, wasn't founded until 1973—now it employs over 5,000 talented people and recruits hundreds per year. The financial services industry has mushroomed in size, with Wall Street firms employing 191,800 at their peak in 2008, up from only 65,300 in 1975.[4] The growth in professional services has given rise to an accompanying set of recruitment pipelines only in the past several decades.

Yet the allocation of talent is a zero-sum game. If the academically gifted are funneled in higher numbers toward finance and consulting, then lesser numbers are going into other areas, such as the operation of companies, startups, and early-stage enterprises. In the United States, companies with fewer than 500 employees account for almost two-thirds of net new jobs and generate thirteen times more new patents per employee than do large firms. If the US economy had generated as many startups each year for 2009–12 as it had in 2007, the country would have produced almost 2.5 million new jobs by 2013.[5] If we're interested in spurring long-term job growth, we want as much talent as possible heading to new firms so that more of them can succeed, expand, and hire more people.

Further, the current talent flows have a pronounced regional bias. The hubs for financial services and consulting are New York, San Francisco, Boston, Chicago, Los Angeles, and Washington, DC, and these cities are magnets for the preponderance of top university graduates. Meanwhile, dozens of other US cities and communities are home to promising growth companies that don't have the talent they need to develop and expand. Companies in Detroit, New Orleans, Las Vegas, Providence, Baltimore, Cleveland, and other cities are poised to hire and to provide new opportunities and products. Yet our national university graduates are being consistently channeled elsewhere.*

Professional services industries like finance, consulting, and legal services are, by definition, meta-industries. That is, they serve to help large companies raise money, buy and sell each other, reorganize, implement new systems, conduct complex transactions, and so forth. They are dependent on companies coming into being and becoming big enough to hire them. The economy needs more companies to start, grow, and thrive in order for the service organizations themselves

---

*One could argue that our national university system has become a de facto talent drain for much of the country. Many states and communities send their top students away to great schools, never to hear from them again.

to prosper. For example, if Mark Zuckerberg had become an investment banker or gone to work in a bank's information technology department, then the bankers wouldn't have had Facebook to take public. It's actually far better for the investment banks (and everyone else) that instead of heading in their direction, he started his own company.

Another issue is that professional paths aren't always the right fit. Everyone reading this knows a host of former lawyers, bankers, consultants, academics, or doctors for whom the work or environment was not right, many of whom eventually left the profession or stuck around halfheartedly. This represents a massive social cost. Instead of an army of bright college graduates, we are left with an array of often indebted former professionals who are only starting years later what should have been their first act. Some find roles that fit. But for most this transition is not seamless; there are often time-consuming stumbles and periods of exploration before a new path is forged or found—if one is found.

Last, and perhaps most important, professional services socialize individuals in ways that are not conducive to their ability to contribute in other ways. All of us, and particularly young people, have a tendency to view ourselves and our natures as static: you'll choose to do something for a few years, and you'll still be the same you. This isn't the case. Spending your twenties traveling four days a week, interviewing employees, and writing detailed reports on how to cut costs will change you, as will spending years editing contracts and arguing about events that will never come to pass, or years producing Excel spreadsheets and moving deals along. After a while, regardless of your initial motivations, your lifestyle and personality will change to fit your role. You will become a better dispenser of well-presented recommendations, or editor of contracts, or generator of financial projections. And you will in all likelihood become less good at other things. You will not be the same person you were when you started.

It is no accident that many of those we regard as our most productive individuals—Bill Gates, Steve Jobs, Jeff Bezos, Howard Schultz, Jack Dorsey, Reid Hoffman, Larry Page, Sergey Brin, and the like—were not products of our professional paths. Michael Dell actually entered the University of Texas intending to go to medical school. He probably would have made a fine doctor. But thanks to him over 100,000 people are now working at his namesake company, both in Texas and around the world.

2

Too Much of a Good Thing

One reason why the hyperallocation of talent to certain industries, regions, and firms goes ignored is that it combines narratives no one wants to talk about.

Our economy has progressed from making things to supplying financial services. It's not the first time an economy has made this transition. Both the Netherlands and Great Britain were global manufacturing powers in their day. The British supplanted the Dutch in the early 1800s. We supplanted the British in the early 1900s. The Dutch and British then turned to financial services and insurance as the drivers of their economies. Unfortunately, it's hard for an economy to rely solely on financial services, and both countries receded from the world stage.[*]

We no longer manufacture devices, we manufacture analyses. Investment banks, private equity firms, corporate law firms, and management consultancies are all vitally impor-

---

[*] For an in-depth discussion of this progression, see Samuel P. Huntington's *The Clash of Civilizations and the Remaking of World Order* (New York: Touchstone, 1996).

tant to today's US economy. They serve crucial roles in helping companies raise capital, get acquired, document complex transactions, and integrate new technologies, among plenty of other necessary tasks.

These types of professional service firms operate in incredibly competitive contexts. Their sustained success hinges on the type of people they have working for them. Everything is honed to a razor's edge. They thus focus assiduously on getting the very smartest people that they can inside their walls. They invest millions in this process and offer prestige, high-starting salaries, training, expense accounts, and the promise of community and open doors.

As one of the cofounders of a major management consulting firm explained it to me,

> We loved to recruit at the top schools because we knew there'd be good hires on campus. It was just a matter of putting resources to work, improving our funnel and tweaking variables until we found them. We would figure out which classes were indicative of intellectual ability and which were just padding, what leadership positions were significant, what majors tended to do well. . . . The more years we spent on campus the better we would get at it. We wanted to get a certain number of recruits from each of our top campuses each year so there would be a constant stream of personal referrals and connections. If we didn't get someone for a few years it was a lot tougher to restart at that school.

It's very admirable and well executed—exactly what you would hope the consulting firm would do if you were a shareholder. But this firm is jockeying for position with dozens of other firms that implement the same sort of process. And before long you have a sort of tragedy of the commons, where the firms are all grazing on the same field to depletion.

To give a sense of the resources being dedicated to this effort, Teach for America's recruitment and selection budget alone in 2011 was $37.6 million. A friend who works in financial services recruiting estimated that her firm spends $50,000 per recruit. If you project the analogous expenditures from every major bank and consulting firm to develop talent pipelines, you have tens if not hundreds of millions being spent each year at major campuses across the country. One hedge fund spends so much on recruitment that it offered to pay Dartmouth students a hundred dollars each to tell the company why they chose *not* to participate in its recruitment process.[1] In 2012, of the four Dartmouth valedictorians, two went to Goldman Sachs, one to Morgan Stanley, and one to McKinsey.[2]

There's an arms race for the best talent at dozens of universities each year. To be clear, no one's at fault. Private firms ought to be doing their utmost to maximize their own well-being. In this case, that means getting on campus, spending time and money, and fighting it out for the top educational prospects in the country. The recruitment culture gives rise to a general pursuit of pathways of prestige as undergrads see those around them heading down well-defined tracks and look to do the same. Most banks and consulting firms make offers between August and December of a student's senior year; imagine being a competitive and slightly insecure senior watching this process unfold around you.

What is the result of this war for talent? Statistics are measured and reported differently, but here's the general picture for top university grads, measured over the last several years of available data.[3]

Postgraduate Pursuits of National University Graduates

	Finance	Consulting	Law	Medicine	Teach for America	Grad School
Harvard	11–17%	7–11%	12–17%	12–16%	4%	8–9%
Yale	10.5–19%	4–14%	15–20%	9–12%	3%	7%
Princeton	22–25%	14–18%	10–15%	9–12%	2%	7–9%
Penn	20–21%	12–13%	11–15%	9–12%	2%	11%
MIT	9–10%	9–10%	1%	7–10%	.6%	29%
Stanford	15%	15%	8–11%	12–16%	2%	
Duke	15–16%	12–14%	12–16%	15–19%	2–3%	4–7%
Brown	8–10%	5–6%	8–12%	10–14%	3%	13–14%
Dartmouth	6–19%	6–12%	12–16%	10–14%	3–4%	3–7%
Cornell	12.3%	7.1%	8–12%	9–13%	1%	20%
Columbia	11–15%	6%	7–10%	7–9%	2%	10–13%
Johns Hopkins	6%	6%	5–8%	18–23%	2%	25%
University of Chicago	7–10%	5–10%	12–15%	6–10%	2%	14–19%
Georgetown	13–16%	7–13%	14–17%	5–8%	3%	11%

Take a minute to survey these numbers. While there's some variation (i.e., more Yale grads go to law school, more people from Johns Hopkins go to med school, and so on), you get a sense that they're all pretty similar in terms of breakdown. As you can see, a literal majority of national university graduates will pursue one of these six paths after graduation, none of which leads directly to new business formation or growth. What begins as a universe of options quickly shrinks to just a few.

I've spoken to hundreds of college seniors who are in this predicament on the front lines. Some examples of the things I heard:

- "If I go to career services, they'll tell me straight out that they only have finance and consulting jobs for me to look at. That or Teach for America."
- "It seems like everywhere you look people are in suits scurrying to another banking interview. It has an effect on you after a while."
- "My friend tried to look for a job at a startup, but it was really difficult. Eventually he gave up and joined a consulting firm."

Some observers mistakenly believe that the recent downturn in financial services and the existence of the movie *The Social Network* mean that the world has changed. But the reality on the ground is determined by which organizations have the resources, brand equity, know-how, time horizon, and consistent and predictable need for new recruits to go on campus and roll out the welcome wagon. These factors have remained more or less constant even after the financial crisis. Though the interest in entrepreneurship is high, most are not acting on their interest. Indeed, according to one McKinsey study, after 2007, eighteen- to twenty-four-year-olds experienced the greatest decline in entrepreneurial activity of any group, leading the authors to conclude, "The US economy is currently not producing enough of its next generation of serial entrepreneurs."[4]

Let's say that you're a small growth company that wants to hire a few top prospects to help fuel your growth. It's not going to be easy. First, you'd have to start trying to hire months in advance, even though your needs may change by the time the hire shows up. You'd have to dedicate scarce staff time and resources to sign up for career fairs, post job descriptions, and show up on campuses that might be several states away. You'd have to compete side by side against name-brand companies with giant displays and well-dressed alumni. You'd have to make a competitive offer against firms that are offering outsize wages and likely recruiting multiple people at once. You'd struggle to get the attention of career services officers because you're probably only looking to hire one or two college seniors. You'd have to evaluate candidates for fit. And after all that, there's little guarantee that you'd actually get your man or woman.

It's a daunting landscape that doesn't serve the little firm very well, so most don't bother trying to go down this road. Yet it's these small firms that will potentially expand, innovate, and hire more and more people if they mature to a certain stage of development.

As recruitment for operating roles diminishes, college seniors are left with a wealth of professional services firms, nonprofit fellowships, and little else. The dearth of options has even bred discontent on campus. In 2011 there were op-eds and articles written by students and alumni at Harvard, Yale, and Stanford bemoaning the prevalence of financial recruiting.[5] One Stanford op-ed in particular was picked up by the national press and inspired a website, Stop the Brain Drain, which protested the flow of talent to Wall Street. The Stanford students wrote,

The financial industry's influence over higher education is deep and multifaceted, including student choice over majors and career tracks, career development resources, faculty and course offerings, and student culture and political activism. In 2010, even after the economic crisis, the financial services industry drew a full 20 percent of Harvard graduates and over 15 percent of Stanford and MIT graduates. This represented the highest portion of any industry except consulting, and about three times more than previous generations.

As the financial industry's profits have increasingly come from complex financial products, like the collateralized debt obligations (CDOs) that ignited the 2008 financial meltdown, its demand has steadily grown for graduates with technical degrees. In 2006, the securities and commodity exchange sector employed a larger portion of scientists and engineers than semiconductor manufacturing, pharmaceuticals and telecommunications.

The result has been a major reallocation of top talent into financial sector jobs, many of which are "socially useless," as the chairman of the United Kingdom's Financial Services Authority put it. This over-allocation reduces the supply of productive entrepreneurs and researchers and damages entrepreneurial capitalism, according to a recent Kauffman Foundation report. Many of these finance jobs contribute to volatile and counter-productive financial speculation. Indeed, Wall Street's activities are largely dominated by speculative security trading and arbitrage instead of investment in new businesses. In 2010, 63 percent of Goldman Sachs' revenue came from trading, compared to only 13 percent from corporate finance.

Why are graduates flocking to Wall Street? Beyond the simple allure of high salaries, investment banks and hedge funds have designed an aggressive, sophisticated, and well-funded recruitment system, which often takes advantage of [a] student's job insecurity. Moreover, elite university culture somehow still upholds finance as a "prestigious" and "savvy" career track.[6]

James Kwak, a successful author who graduated from Harvard and later worked at the top consulting firm McKinsey and Company before attending law school, writes about the recruitment and acculturation process,

The typical Harvard undergraduate is someone who: (a) is very good at school; (b) has been very successful by conventional standards for his entire life; (c) has little or no experience of the "real world" outside of school or school-like settings; (d) feels either the ambition or the duty to have a positive impact on the world (not well defined); and (e) is driven more by fear of not being a success than by a concrete desire to do anything in particular. (Yes, I know this is a stereotype; that's why I said "typical.") Their (our) decisions are motivated by two main decision rules: (1) close down as few options as possible; and (2) only do things that increase the possibility of future overachievement. Money is far down the list; at this point in their lives, if you asked them, many of these people would probably say that they only need to be middle or upper middle class, and assume that they will be.

The recruiting processes of Wall Street firms (and consulting firms, and corporate law firms) exploit these (faulty)

decision rules perfectly. The primary selling point of Goldman Sachs or McKinsey is that it leaves open the possibility of future greatness. The main pitch is, "Do this for two years, and afterward you can do anything (like be treasury secretary)." The idea is that you will get some kind of generic business training that equips you to do anything (this in a society that assumes the private sector can do no wrong and the public sector can do no right), and that you will get the résumé credentials and connections you need to go on and do whatever you want. And to some extent it's true, because these names look good on your résumé, and very few potential future employers will wonder why you decided to go there. (Whether the training is good for much other than being a banker or a consultant is another question.)

The second selling point is that they make it easy. Yes, there is competition for jobs at these firms. But the process is easy. They come to campus and hold receptions with open bars. They tell you when and how to apply. They provide interview coaching. They have nice people who went to your school bond with you over the recruiting period. If you get an offer, they find out what your other options are and have partners call you to explain that those are great options, but Goldman/McKinsey is better, and you can do that other thing later, anyway. For people who don't know how to get a job in the open economy, and who have ended each phase of their lives by taking the test to do the most prestigious thing possible in the next phase, all of this comes naturally. (Graduate schools, which also have well-defined recruiting processes, are the other big path to take.) The fact that most companies don't want new college graduates makes it easier to go to one of the few that do.

The third selling point—not the top one, but it's there—is the money. Or, more accurately, the lifestyle. The glossy brochures never say how much money you can make. But they make it clear that you will be part of the well-dressed, well-fed, jet-setting elite. When people walk into those offices, with fresh flowers and all-glass walls and free food and modern technology everywhere, they get seduced. Last summer one person wrote to my school's e-mail list about how wonderful his office was, with its view of Central Park. I mentioned this to an old friend who used to work at McKinsey, and he said, "He fell for the office. . . ."

And once you're in the door, the seduction begins. . . .

It's just human nature. Your expenses grow to match your income. As the decades pass and you realize that no, you're not going to save the world, the money becomes a more and more important part of the justification. And when you have kids, you're stuck; it's much easier to deprive yourself of money (and what it buys) than to deprive your children of money.

More important, you internalize the rationalizations for the work you are doing. It's easier to think that underwriting new debt offerings really is saving the world than to think that you are underwriting new debt offerings, because of the money, instead of saving the world. And this goes for many walks of life. It's easier for college professors to think that, by training the next generation of young minds (or, even more improbably, writing papers on esoteric subjects), they are changing the world than to think that they are teaching and researching instead of changing the world.

Sure, there are self-parodying, economically delusional, psychotherapy-needing, despicable people on Wall Street . . .

but there are also a lot of people who went there because it was easy and stayed because they decided they couldn't afford not to and talked themselves into it.

A college student asked me at a book talk what I thought about undergraduates who go work on Wall Street. And individually, I have nothing against them, although I do think they should do their best to keep their expenses down so they will be able to switch careers later. But as a system, it's a bad thing that a small handful of highly profitable firms are able to invest those profits into skimming off some of the top students at American universities—universities that, even if nominally private, are partially funded by taxpayer money in the form of research grants and federal subsidies for student loans—and absorbing them into the banking-consulting-lawyering Borg.[7]

Ezra Klein of the *Washington Post* conducted an interview with a Harvard grad who'd studied history, government, and political philosophy before going to Wall Street. Her responses reflect a similar perspective on how many of these decisions are made:

Investment banking was never something I thought I wanted to do. But the recruiting culture at Harvard is extremely powerful. In the midst of anxiety and trying to find a job at the end of college, the recruiters are really in your face, and they make it very easy. . . . if [your internship] goes well, you have an offer by September of your senior year, and that's very appealing. It makes your senior year more relaxed, you can focus on your thesis, you can drink more. You just don't have to worry about getting a job.

And separate from that, I think it's about squelching anxiety in general. It checks the job box. And it's a low-risk opportunity. It's a two-year program with a great salary and the promise to get these skills that should be able to transfer to a variety of other areas. The idea is that once you pass the test at Goldman, you can do anything. You learn Excel, you learn valuation, you learn how to survive intense hours and a high-pressure environment. So it seems like a good way to launch your career. That's very appealing for those of us at Harvard who were not in pre-professional majors. . . .

These aren't the types of things you grow up dreaming of doing, but you wear a business suit, you meet clients. It's a way of growing up very quickly. And investment banking has the added advantage that you can make money very quickly and afford a great apartment in New York, which is very expensive. . . .

Private equity firms were trying to recruit us in the first year of my two-year training program. There's this notion of the accidental banker, people who get caught up in that world and get more and more pay and find it harder to justify leaving. But the cultural effect of all of this—and even with regulatory reform, we need to think about that—is that a lot of people decide to sacrifice much more time than they normally would because the money is so good, and then they believe they deserve extremely high pay because they're giving up so much time. It's not malicious. But there are a lot of unhappy people who end up in that situation.[8]

We have reached the evolutionary stage of our economy at which a number of things are happening that have never happened before. Thanks to the institutions and individuals that have preceded us (and lately, some loose Federal Reserve policy), mountains of capital are now available, as well as a massive industry dedicated to managing and allocating this capital. This industry can pay better than any other. Corporate complexity has given rise to a similarly massive management consulting industry. Economic rationality is driving both firms and individuals toward certain outcomes that threaten our long-term growth.

A Kauffman Foundation study published in 2011 concluded that because financial instruments have become more complex, "the [financial] industry now focuses its recruiting on new master's- and doctoral-level graduates of science, engineering, math and physics, and pays them starting wages that are five times or more what they would have earned had they remained in their own fields. Because these new hires are often the very individuals who otherwise would have comprised the most robust pool of prospective founders of high-growth companies, the financial services industry's steady rise has had a cannibalizing effect on entrepreneurship in the U.S. economy."[9]

Translation: finance is now recruiting and throwing money at the very smart technical people who would have been among the most likely to start businesses, reducing the number of startups over time.

I had drinks with a friend who runs a trading desk at a large multinational bank who was trained as an engineer. He said, "Even I think recruiting PhDs from Caltech to write trading algorithms for my desk is a little wrong. I feel like they should be working on the mission to Mars or something." But it's not going to keep him from recruiting them and offering very lucrative compensation packages.

I met a woman who was completing her PhD in biology at Harvard. She mentioned that the only two firms that actively recruited from her program were not pharmaceutical companies or biotech startups; instead, they were the two leading consulting firms, McKinsey and Company and the Boston Consulting Group. The new highest use of a PhD in biology is not to be in the lab; it is to conduct analyses of large drug companies.

The Stanford students and others appealed to the universities themselves to somehow address this situation. Administrators are privately sympathetic; universities don't fancy themselves as simply de facto training grounds for bankers and consultants. In 2008, Drew Gilpin Faust, the president of Harvard, gave a commencement speech to graduating seniors asking them to transcend Wall Street's "all but irresistible recruiting juggernaut." Princeton is looking for a new director of career services who will open up a wider variety of options for its liberal arts grads. But university departments are ill-equipped to intervene, as career services offices primarily organize incoming outreach from employers. Career services offices are somewhat understandably subject to the institutions that deploy resources to recruit their students. There is literally a Goldman Sachs Room in Columbia's career services office where students go for information sessions. And it would be completely unrealistic for a university to limit the private companies that are coming to campus to offer their graduates high-salaried jobs; for many, that's the whole point of attending the school.

A handful of professors have attempted to give students alternatives on their own. Evan Korth and Chris Wiggins, professors of computer science and applied math at NYU and Columbia, respectively, got tired of seeing their students head to Wall Street banks every year. Indeed, one venture capital firm's research showed that only 13 percent of computer science graduates at the top East Coast schools went to startups in recent years.[10] Evan and Chris, along with technologist Hilary Mason, started hackNY in 2010 to place promising programmers at New York–based startups; its declared mission is "to keep kids off the Street." When I spoke with them, Wiggins said, "New York City has had a very strong economy in financial services and the road to finance became well traveled." Korth added, "What we wanted to build is a network of talented young developers—hackers in the sense of creative problem solvers—who could learn from each other while building and sustained a strong tech community." The hackNY program has trained over one hundred programmers and funneled them into tech companies. As admirable as this effort is, hackNY's singularity and the fact that college professors felt the need to start an organization for this purpose speaks volumes.

How do we increase the odds of individuals taking on the challenges of starting or working at a new business? We are growing increasingly reliant upon outliers, people who are intrinsically superenterprising and relatively ignorant of economic incentives. And many of the people who would have the most to offer as a founder or inventor simply have other more directly appealing options.

3

Professional Training Cuts Both Ways

I often get asked these questions from young people who are considering going to law school: "Do you use your law degree in what you do? Has it helped you?"

These are difficult questions to answer succinctly. It's impossible for me to say that it doesn't play into my day-to-day activities because law school and briefly practicing law rewired my brain. I'm more structured and detail-oriented than I would have been. Having gone to law school years ago still impacts my job performance every day.

Plus, people tended to accord me some professional respect in my twenties in part because I had a high-value graduate degree. It would be disingenuous not to acknowledge the impact it's had.

On the other hand, it's not as if I'm editing contracts or figuring out if something is legal on a regular basis. If I were to come across a genuine legal issue I'd call a lawyer who specializes in that sort of thing or look it up online like anyone else.

Legal training (and the subsequent indebtedness) would

not be my first suggestion to a young person looking to do something enterprising.* I felt I had to unlearn a lot as I embarked down a very different road.

As we've seen, one of the most frequently pursued paths for achievement-minded college seniors is to spend several years advancing professionally and getting trained and paid by an investment bank, consulting firm, or law firm. Then, the thought process goes, they can set out to do something else with some exposure and experience under their belts. People are generally not making lifelong commitments to the field in their own minds. They're "getting some skills" and making some connections before figuring out what they really want to do.

I subscribed to a version of this mind-set when I graduated from Brown. In my case, I went to law school thinking I'd practice for a few years (and pay down my law school debt) before lining up another opportunity.

It's clear why this is such an attractive approach. There are some immensely constructive things about spending several years in professional services after graduating from college. Professional service firms are designed to train large groups of recruits annually, and they do so very successfully. After even just a year or two in a high-level bank or consulting firm, you emerge with a set of skills that can be applied in other contexts (financial modeling in Excel if you're a financial analyst, PowerPoint and data organization and presentation if you're a consultant, and editing and issue spotting

---

*Here's a list of required law school courses I took: civil procedure, torts, contracts, foundations of legal thought, the regulatory state, constitutional law, criminal law, property. Studying these things might make you smarter, but there aren't many businesses that relate to these subjects.

if you're a lawyer). This is very appealing to most any recent graduate who may not yet feel equipped with practical skills coming right out of college.

Even more than the professional skill you gain, if you spend time at a bank, consultancy, or law firm, you will become excellent at producing world-class work. Every model, report, presentation, or contract needs to be sophisticated, well done, and error free, in large part because that's one of the core value propositions of your organization. The people above you will push you to become more rigorous and disciplined, and your work product will improve across the board as a result. You'll get used to dressing professionally, preparing for meetings, speaking appropriately, showing up on time, writing official correspondence, and so forth. You will be able to speak the corporate language. You'll become accustomed to working very long hours doing detail-intensive work. These attributes are transferable to and helpful in many other contexts.

In many of these roles you'll be exposed to the problems and features of particular industries. In finance you might do deals within the media sector, so you'll have a chance to become familiar with different media companies. In consulting, maybe you'll be serving insurance companies that are consolidating or adopting new software systems. This exposure can make you more valuable and marketable to firms in that industry; it can also give you a more sophisticated grasp of the problems big companies face.

You will learn to appreciate how detailed processes are necessary for most large organizations to function properly. Your confidence will grow as you gain exposure to decision makers and top-flight professionals. As you spend more time at a big-name firm, you will get a sense of the sort of people who populate and succeed in these environments. They're your friends and colleagues (and you). You're likely to gain the impression that you've worked among some of the best in a field and that you're as capable as anyone else.

Similarly, your experience at a big firm is a great signal to prospective employers and partners. It will give you a source of credibility with clients, investors, and anyone else you deal with for the rest of your career. You will almost always leave a professional services environment with a few noteworthy friends and relationships; these contacts can prove to be extremely valuable both personally and professionally.

And it's true, some people who come out of these firms are ideally motivated and hungry. They've seen the other side, and now they want to build something and make a mark. They're not afraid to work hard. They're determined to achieve something significant outside of their old context.

It seems like an incredible set of benefits. How can there be any downside to either the individual or to the economy that a significant proportion of our top graduates head down these roads?

Unfortunately, there are some potential trade-offs to consider, particularly if you are hoping to take a professional services experience and apply it later to working at or even starting a small company.

In professional service environments, the output is almost always analytical—a set of valuations for a company, a series of cost-cutting recommendations, or the optimal way to organize an acquisition for tax purposes. The question is, "How much is this company worth?" or "How do we manage our supply chain better to save us millions of dollars?" Sometimes an analysis can take months to generate, with a half dozen people working on it for hundreds of hours.

In the startup setting and in most small companies, the output is action-oriented. You're not an analyst; you're the operator. You need to get things done and make decisions, often with limited information and resources. You need to hire people, devise and improve a product, get customers and drum up business, market your service and the company, fulfill orders and provide customer service, learn how to manage and lead a team (when they're not all either analysts or support staff), and allocate what little money you have.

For most small companies, the value is in the execution. You push in a particular direction and find out if you're right in real time, and then change approaches accordingly. Mistakes are acceptable if they're the result of moving forward (whereas in the professional services context mistakes are regarded very negatively). It's less about strategy and more about did you make your customer(s) happy today? or did you get paid? You develop judgment and instincts around execution that are very different from what is sometimes jokingly called "analysis paralysis." Examining a company, valuing it, or making recommendations about it are activities that are very different from those involved in operating it.

Much has been made about how companies struggle to innovate and challenge themselves if they have a business that is successful.[*] People function the same way. If you're a young professional making over $150,000 per year producing

---

[*] Clayton Christensen's *Innovator's Dilemma* spells this out in compelling detail.

spreadsheets, analyses, recommendations, and/or contracts, it's extraordinarily difficult to then switch to doing something else and starting from scratch. I've seen many people leave positions to try their hands in another arena, only to get discouraged with the lack of pay and the slow path to success, particularly when they're competing with people who have been engaged in that new activity for years. Meanwhile, it's a relatively narrow band of opportunities that will pay you at the same level as your current job. It's harder to take on the struggle when there's another path waiting with a bag of money.

I had a friend who was a brilliant writer. He went to law school, became a corporate attorney at a top firm, and then discovered he disliked it. So he quit to become a screenwriter. After months of writing and shopping a couple of scripts around, he hadn't made the kind of progress he'd envisioned. So he became a lawyer at another firm to pay the bills while still holding out hope that he could make a career for himself creatively. Years passed. He's now a senior structured-finance lawyer.

I know, no one feels particularly bad for a highly paid professional—but this shows how it can be tough to transition out. This situation is referred to as having "golden handcuffs," which sounds ridiculous until you see it up close. A job is more than a job—it's your car, how you dress, where you live, the relationships you have, and many other things. It's unrealistic to think that one can adopt a certain lifestyle for several years and then make an abrupt change without having to make other significant adjustments.

Contrary to popular belief, exciting companies are not generally reaching out to banking analysts, consultants, or corporate lawyers with great opportunities. Startups, for example, often hire from within personal networks and take on people who are actively engaged in the startup community. Most small- to medium-size companies need one finance wizard, not twelve of them, and they may already have someone with financial acumen on the senior team. Headhunters are eager to place you at another investment bank, consulting firm, or law firm, or perhaps in an in-house position at a large company, but they almost always stick to the same role (it'd be a tougher sell for them to try and help people switch; plus, the commission would be smaller). This is exacerbated by the fact that, for many professionals, engaging in a conventional job search is something they've never done; most were recruited directly out of school.

I saw this happen dozens of times when I was teaching investment banking analysts and junior management consultants. They struggled to figure out the next step. Many couldn't find the right fit, gave up after a year or two, and applied to business school, which they hoped would lead them to the ideal opportunity.[*]

---

[*] Meanwhile, the majority of business school grads return to financial services and management consulting. For example, in 2012, 60 percent of Harvard MBAs went to work in the financial services sector (35 percent) or management consulting (25 percent; see Harvard Business School, "Employment Statistics," retrieved from http://www.hbs.edu/recruiting/mba/data-and-statistics/employment-statistics.html). The proportion of top MBA students who have interned at a startup or growth company or tried to start one themselves during the summer before their second year remains very low (e.g., 9 percent at Wharton, 13 percent at Harvard, and 9 percent at Stanford in 2012), and many of these students go on to take more stable corporate jobs after graduation; see Erin Zlomek, "MBAs Forgo Summer Internships for Startup Work," *Bloomberg Businessweek*, retrieved from http://www.businessweek.com/articles/2013-04-18/mbas-forgo-summer-internships-for-startup-work.

The skills developed in finance, consulting, and law are valuable in certain contexts, but most businesses revolve around some other central activity like software, retail, energy, health care, or media. Many professionals become specialized in analytical positions and don't have a chance to develop in ways that would make them more central to building or driving a business.

If you ask a consultant what he or she wants to do at your company, the answer will likely be, "I want to determine your strategy." If you ask a banker, it may be, "I want to be your CFO." Meanwhile, most companies don't need a new strategy and aren't about to go public; their day-to-day concerns revolve around personnel, improving their offerings, making customers happy, and getting more business.* A company needs to become quite sizable before the idea of taking on a banker or consultant begins to make sense.

The nature of professional services dictates that you work on a deal or a client engagement that lasts a brief period and then ends. You're usually staffed on a deal that will last for a finite period until the deal either comes through or falls apart. You begin a new transaction or client engagement every several months, perhaps longer if it's a protracted consulting project. You're used to relationships measured in weeks or months, or only hours or minutes in the trading context. Clients arrive and demand a flurry of activity until

---

*In particular, a move to drive sales is the lifeblood of most small businesses. Presenting, which many professionals are excellent at, is not exactly selling. *Presenting* means there's a logo and a dozen people sitting in the boardroom waiting to hear what you have to say. *Selling* means trying to get someone's attention about your little company—one they've never heard of.

a transaction is complete, then disappear. Senior managers at your firm maintain relationships with clients, but you're a level or two removed.

You often develop strong relationships with colleagues due to the long hours, extensive travel, and intense work environment. But you're used to people coming and going very quickly as teams either shift and change or people leave the firm. For example, the attrition rate at one top consulting firm is 30 percent per year, which is one reason they're always hiring.[1]

The constant flow of different deals is presented as a selling point by many consulting firms and investment banks. They'll say it's "fast-paced," things are "changing all the time," and that you'll work on one deal or project "and then move on."

Most operating companies, in contrast, typically rely upon long-term relationships to function well. They require a significant commitment in which the time frame is measured in years, not weeks or months. Turnover is detrimental to developing a good management team; building a business, and building up the value of one's equity and relationships within an industry, takes time.

As a professional service provider who is changing clients or transactions every period, it's hard to become emotionally invested in your work. It's like trying to be concerned about taking care of a car you're renting. Your clients are themselves big companies, and your interaction with them will often be limited to the occasional meeting with a senior executive or a manager. If you're a consultant, you're generally set up in a conference room from Monday through Thursday in a far-flung city; then you fly home on Thursday night. You're there as a transaction cost because someone wants to get something done.

One ex-consultant I interviewed noted, "It's hard to get personally attached or invested when you know you're only there for a number of months. I had assignments and deliverables that I knew would get changed after six months because we were a stopgap solution—I knew my work would disappear in a little while after the new system was put in."

Your appetite for risk generally diminishes as you get older. This can become even more pronounced in a professional setting. You spend your working life in nice offices around well-compensated people. You often have support staff from day one. The only people you interact with work at large public companies. Your expenses creep upward over time, and you get used to having nice things. Your interpersonal obligations mount, and the people you're dating and family members expect you to earn lots of money. As you adapt to your role and circumstance, taking a risk professionally becomes more and more of an abstraction.

Once, while I was having drinks with a friend of mine after she started working at a top-tier consulting firm, she said, "Before I got here, I thought I could do anything. Now, I feel like you can't do anything unless you have a budget of millions of dollars."

In the minds of college seniors, and thanks to prodigious investment on the part of the firms themselves, professional services—financial services and management consulting—have become conflated with "business" when really they're a narrow subset or category of businesses with distinctive features.

If you work in professional services you will be paid handsomely and have a brand-name firm on your résumé. You'll gain skills, confidence, and exposure. But you may also become heavily socialized and specialized, more risk averse, and accustomed to operating in resource-rich environments with a narrow set of deliverables. You'll be likely to adopt an arm's-length relationship with your work. You won't build anything; instead, you will compartmentalize and put the armor on each day as deals, clients, and colleagues come and go.

Professional services are being used as a de facto training ground for our top college graduates—with mixed results for everyone concerned. In particular, going into banking or consulting to learn how to start or run a business is not always ideal; the processes are very different, and give you a sense of companies trying to do different things. It's like trying to learn how to become a chef by going to a company that runs analyses for large restaurant chains. Yes, you'll get a better grasp of how chain restaurants work. But will you learn to cook?

There are, of course, any number of successful business builders and entrepreneurs who started out as professionals, as one would expect given that literally half our top graduates have pursued these paths for the past couple decades. David Gilboa worked at an investment bank before cofounding Warby Parker. John Delbridge worked in equity research before cofounding Mimeo. People have long careers that aren't defined by their first few years.

And it's easy to get excited about a potential hire if he has spent a couple of years at a top firm. There's a good chance that this person is smart, motivated, capable of long hours and detail-oriented work, and is looking for a change. If applying to work at a startup, he probably expects a pay cut and has the right motivation.

But if I had a dollar for all the bankers, consultants, and lawyers I've met who told me that they were "really interested in entrepreneurship," I'd be awfully rich. Meanwhile, they struggle to transition into different roles, and many of them have lost some of the qualities that would have enabled them to take on their original ambitions.

Their problem isn't just theirs—it affects all of us. We're breeding large battalions of indifferent professionals in a handful of cities when what we need is something very different. We need committed builders.

I had several friends from law school who were very enterprising guys, much more so than the average law student. They each started businesses after practicing law at large firms for multiple years. What kind of businesses did they start? They started boutique law firms.

This is completely unsurprising if you think about it. They'd spent years becoming good at delivering legal services. It was a field that they understood and could compete in. Their credentials translated too.

People learn from what they're doing and do it again on their own. It's not just lawyers; the consulting firm Bain and Company was started by seven former partners and managers from the Boston Consulting Group. Myriad boutique investment banks and hedge funds have spun out of large financial organizations.

You can see the same pattern in the startup world. After PayPal was acquired by eBay in 2002, its founders and employees went on to found or cofound LinkedIn (Reid Hoffman), YouTube (Steve Chen, Jawed Karim, and Chad Hurley), Yelp (Russel Simmons and Jeremy Stoppelman), Tesla Motors (Elon Musk), SpaceX (Musk again), Yammer (David Sacks), 500 Startups (Dave McClure), and many other companies. PayPal's CEO, Peter Thiel, famously made a $500,000 investment in Facebook that grew to over $1 billion.

In this sense, PayPal is one of the most prolific companies of recent times. But if you look at any successful growth company you'll start to see their alumni show up doing parallel things. Former Apple employees founded or cofounded Android, Palm, Nest, and Handspring, companies that revolve around devices. Former Yahoo! employees founded Ycombinator, Cloudera, Hunch.com, AppNexus, Polyvore, and many other web-oriented companies. Organizations give rise to other organizations like themselves.

A successful startup or growth company will begin channeling talent, money, know-how, resources, and culture into its environment. People who have done it will do it again.

4

Network Effects and Why Human Capital Markets Don't Self-Correct

Let's say that you were to line up a hundred brilliant twenty-one-year-olds who might have the potential to start a company someday. You tell them, "Okay, you have two choices. You can commit to being an entrepreneur and start a company. There's a ten percent chance that you become extraordinarily successful, wealthy, and create hundreds of jobs. There's a twenty-five percent chance that you're a modest success. And there's a sixty-five percent chance that you toil in obscurity for years and your confidence diminishes, potentially damaging your attractiveness to potential mates even if you later become more conventional. Alternatively, you can commit to a high-paying career at a well-regarded company, and there's a ninety-five percent chance you'll succeed by most conventional standards."

What would these one hundred brilliant twenty-one-year-olds do? Most of them would probably opt for the latter path, because they only have one outcome to consider—their own. They have one life to live, and both the chances of failure and the consequences may come across as unacceptably high. These individuals have often been successful at whatever they've put their minds to up to this point, which may make taking on risks unappealing. Plus, their parents likely invested considerable resources getting them to this point, increasing the pressure to ensure a return. And they're confident that they'll get dates, learn things, be around other smart people, and make lots of money at a name-brand firm, regardless of their other ambitions.

Let's change the scenario a little bit. What would happen if you were to line up the same twenty-one-year-olds and have them all spend two years working together and becoming friends? Then you give them the same choice, but with this change: "You will all agree that if you become an extraordinarily successful entrepreneur, you will share the rewards with the other ninety-nine people in this room by hiring as many of them for your venture as you can." Would this change anything?

Now, each person's risk would be significantly reduced as long as someone in the cohort does extremely well. As long as one person becomes Jeff Bezos, the downside risk is a position as vice president of something or other at Amazon. That doesn't seem bad at all. Taking the risky path may be a more reasonable bet for each as a result of the collective understanding.

One way to get a greater number of our most talented young people to embark on the higher-risk, higher-reward path would be to create a community and network oriented around starting new enterprises. It's a lot easier to take risks if you're part of a group whose members will look out for each other.

There's a country that does something a little like this.

Its young people, including its very best educational prospects from all different backgrounds, spend two or three years training and solving problems in a nonhierarchical environment and get together every year. Many then collaborate to start companies. This country leads the world in venture capital investments per capita (over $170, versus $75 in the United States in 2010).[1] It has more companies on the NASDAQ than any non-US country except for China, despite having a population of less than eight million.[2] Its quarterly gross domestic product (GDP) growth rate was above 5 percent in 2011 and it's in the top thirty globally in per capita GDP, above Spain and Saudi Arabia, among others.[3]

This country is Israel, where eighteen-year-olds complete two- or three-year tours in the military, getting to know each other in highly selective military units. They operate at a high level of autonomy and responsibility and then travel the world for months before heading to college and/or grad school. In Dan Senor and Saul Singer's book *Start-up Nation*, this network and training ground is credited as helping give rise to a culture of risk taking and entrepreneurship. By the time Israelis graduate from college, they're in their midtwenties and mature; in many cases, they've already been in operating environments and borne life-and-death responsibilities.

This cocktail of experience gives rise to a mixture of both courage and impatience. As one entrepreneur put it, "When an Israeli entrepreneur has a business idea, he will start it that week. The notion that one should accumulate credentials before launching a venture simply does not exist. . . . Too much time can only teach you what can go wrong, not what could be transformative."[4] Another observer commented, "Israelis . . . don't care about the social price of failure and they develop their projects regardless of the economic . . . situation."[5]

In the United States, many college seniors have been students continuously for seventeen years, with their professional experience limited to a summer internship or two. Four-year graduation rates at elite US schools are very high (90 percent for Georgetown and Notre Dame, 89 percent for Yale and Columbia, and so on), demonstrating that most top students are finishing college without significant interruption.[6] It's not surprising that it might be natural for these graduates to continue to keep their heads down and seek the next step of advancement at every turn, particularly if they were reared in an era of hypercompetitive college admissions.[7] A group of college educators and administrators has observed that "the pressures on today's students seem far more intense than those placed on previous generations. . . . Even 'play-time' is often structured and enriched with just the right mix. . . . Summer vacations have become a thing of the past. . . . By high school the pressure intensifies. Students start to specialize in one activity even to the exclusion of other pursuits . . . the 'right' graduate school looms after college, and the 'right' sequence of jobs is next."[8] This culture of perpetual advancement fosters the opposite of the Israeli risk-taking I-don't-care-about-the-social-cost-of-failure attitude.

If we want to encourage a greater variety of postgraduate pursuits, we should give our young people time to look up and explore different options during their college careers.

While requiring national service along the lines of the Israel Defense Forces is unlikely, working in different environments for a year or more would give students a sense of how their schoolwork intersects with what they might want to do in the long term.* This in turn could make their goals more diverse and independent.

A friend of mine, Neetu, was a top student in Canada. She participated in a cooperative industry education program that had her take the equivalent of a year off between her sophomore and junior years in college. She spent four months working as a marketing associate and youth industry intern for the Calgary Immigrant Aid Society. Then she spent eight months as a business development researcher at a large oil and gas company. Neetu realized that she preferred the private sector because of the higher efficiency and ability to get things done. She took another semester off to intern at a small advertising and design firm. Her experiences influenced how she approached her studies during her senior year in college and how they would be applied in the real world. She began sitting in on advanced courses and joined a marketing club. When she graduated, she went to work as a marketing and communications specialist at an education

---

* The most significant effort to call for large-scale civilian national service is the Aspen Institute's Franklin Project, led by General Stanley McChrystal and made public in June 2013. Another entrepreneur recently suggested a national service program for college-bound students and argued that "the reason college graduates don't know what it's like to work is because they study twenty hours a week and they have their life in college managed for them. . . . they are getting a warped perspective of what life is like." Evan Burfield, quoted in Jeff Selingo, *College (Un)bound: The Future of Education and What It Means for Students* (Boston: Houghton Mifflin Harcourt, 2013), 166.

tech company called Smart Technologies, which she became connected to through a recommendation from the design firm. Smart Technologies went public three years later, in 2010. Neetu credits her year off with both making her studies more productive and giving her more insight into what sort of work and work environment she'd enjoy.

Cooperative programs like the one Neetu participated in are something of a rarity in the United States. If this changed, perhaps our college grads' choices would change as well. The impact would be compounded if we had people spend months in teams operating and solving problems as the Israelis do; they'd emerge with not only a broader perspective but also with relationships they could call on when it's time to build something.

Instead, we emphasize greater schooling, with a mammoth assumption that the market will arrive at the appropriate nature and amount for the available opportunities. Unfortunately, for a number of reasons, human capital markets don't work quite that well.

Let's take the case of US law schools as an example. If you were to say to someone educated, "There are too many law schools producing too many lawyers in the US," she would probably agree, in part because there have been dozens of articles over the past several years about the precipitous drop in positions at law firms and the many unemployed law school graduates.[9] The general response to this problem is, "Well, people will figure it out and eventually stop applying to law school," the suggestion being that the market will clear and self-correct if given enough time.

On the surface it looks like this market magic is now

happening. In 2013, law school applications are projected to be down to about 54,000 from a high of 98,700 in 2004.[10] That's a dramatic decrease of 45 percent.

However, a closer look shows that the number of students who started law school in 2011 and are set to graduate in 2014 was 48,697, about 43,000 of whom will graduate, based on historical graduation rates.[11] We'll still be producing 36,000–43,000 newly minted law school grads a year, not far from the peak of 44,495 set in 2012, from now until the current entering class graduates in 2016. Meanwhile, in 2011, only 65.4 percent of law school graduates got jobs for which they needed to pass the bar exam, and estimates of the number of new legal jobs available run as low as 2,180 per year.[12] *Bloomberg Businessweek* has projected a surplus of 176,000 unemployed or underemployed law school graduates by 2020.[13] So even as applications plummet, there will not be dramatically fewer law school graduates produced in the coming several years, though it will have been easier to get in as acceptance rates rise due to the diminished applicant pool.[14] We'll still be producing many more lawyers than the market requires, but now they'll be less talented. If anything, the situation is going to get worse before it gets better.

Human capital markets don't self-correct very quickly, if at all. At a minimum there's a massive time lag that spans years, for several reasons.

First, there's an information gap. There's generally a five- or six-year age difference between those who are considering attending a school or graduate program and those who have graduated and been out in the working world for any length of time. The average twenty-two-year-old will not have consistent enough access to people who have recently graduated from a program to be able to get a sense of their experience.[15] Parents, who play key roles in these decisions, are similarly relying upon decades-old impressions.

Even if you get ahold of a twenty-eight-year-old graduate, it's not in his or her self-interest to say, "Hey, this school I attended was a waste of time and money. I'm badly indebted. Don't go here." This would make the twenty-eight-year-old seem like a chump. It's much more likely for him or her to put on a brave face and say it's good for some things and not others. A lot of the discussion depends upon things like salaries, debt load, and career prospects. People aren't likely to share these details with others. Most people don't even tell their family members what their credit profile looks like.

Also, the time lag is long enough that people believe current experiences might not apply to them. You're projecting employment trends three or four years from now; if you're looking to pursue a particular ambition you can easily project an improved climate several years in the future.

People often have personal reasons to attend a program that are based not on economics but on identity. They want that degree to become a lawyer, chef, or artist. It's a decision that transcends rational calculations. This is compounded by the fact that most major education expenses are not paid for out-of-pocket but are instead financed by debt that doesn't need to be repaid until years later.*

---

*US student loan debt recently surpassed $1 trillion, with $110 billion borrowed in 2011 alone, much of it supported by the federal government. Fifty million Americans now have a student loan, slightly more than the number of people on Medicare and almost as many as receive Social Security benefits. See Jeff Selingo, *College (Un)bound: The Future of Higher Education and What It Means for Students* (Boston: Houghton Mifflin Harcourt, 2013), xiv.

Complicating matters further is that there's a personal bias toward overconfidence. Even if someone hears that only 20 percent of graduates from a particular school get a good job, he will think, "Okay, I just need to finish in the top twenty percent. No problem." The issue is that 80 percent will think the same thing, and three-quarters of them will wind up being wrong. Everyone's making a decision based on his or her individual situation and interests, which leads to a collective imbalance.

So no, the market will not self-correct for lawyers. We will continue to produce thousands of surplus law school graduates for the foreseeable future, despite secular changes that suggest that the legal job market is unlikely to return to its earlier form.[*] My friends who are law school professors will likely continue to live well. Administrators will shorten programs, some marginal schools will close, and some faculty positions will disappear, but the imbalance won't change unless there is massive reform, which will be forced upon law schools if applications eventually drop below 40,000 per year.[†]

---

[*]Routine legal work is increasingly outsourced offshore, outsourced to contract attorneys, or performed by professionals who do not have a juris doctor degree. See Victor Fleischer, "The Shift Toward Law School Specialization," *New York Times*, October 25, 2012, retrieved from http://dealbook.nytimes.com/2012/10/25/the-shift-toward-law-school-specialization/. There are also new technologies putting lawyers out of work, including software that can do tedious document-review projects that used to require an actual human. See Adam Cohen, "Just How Bad Off Are Law School Graduates?" *Time*, March 11, 2013, retrieved from http://ideas.time.com/2013/03/11/just-how-bad-off-are-law-school-graduates/.

[†]Law schools are huge profit centers for most universities, and they subsidize other departments. See, e.g., Joe Palazzolo and Carmen Phipps, "With Profession under Stress, Law Schools Cut Admissions," *Wall Street*

People often invoke market dynamics when these talent allocation problems are discussed, assuming that market magic will kick in and all will be well. If there are too many of one thing or too few of another, it will correct itself if we ignore it long enough. Too many PhDs and not enough jobs for them?* People will figure it out. Too many of some things and not enough startups? Let's wait for the next recession and it will fix itself.

I'm an American, and I love and respect markets as much as the next guy. But this magical thinking is naive and ineffective. In a downturn, companies will spend a bit less on recruitment, but the current dynamics will still apply. Law school is easily the most stark example of how the market won't realign. Everyone can agree that there's an imbalance and we can see that it's not sorting itself out, impacting tens of thousands of people a year (and likely costing taxpayers millions down the road if graduates are unable to pay off their student loans). You can't counter decades of socializa-

---

Journal, June 11, 2012, retrieved from http://online.wsj.com/article/SB10 001424052702303444204577458411514818378.html. It's very hard for an administrator to voluntarily reduce his or her own budget or enrollment. Plus, the dean could rightfully say that it's not as if one law school reducing its size would solve the problem when there are another two hundred law schools that are accredited by the American Bar Association.

*The proportion of new PhDs from American universities that don't have positions after graduation is now between 25 to 40 percent, depending upon the discipline. This surplus is referred to in education circles as "the PhD Problem," as tenure track positions dwindle but the number of PhDs continues to grow. See Jordan Weissman, "The PhD Bust: America's Awful Job Market for Young Scientists—in 7 Charts," *Atlantic*, Feb. 20, 2013, retrieved from http://www.theatlantic.com/business/archive/2013/02/the-phd-bust-americas-awful-market-for-young-scientists-in-7-charts/273339/.

tion and millions of dollars in branding and recruitment with nothing and expect young people to embrace the void. If you want to solve a problem, you actually have to solve the problem.*

So what's the alternative? That's what the next part is about.

---

*The ideal way to create demand for lawyers would be to have hundreds of entrepreneurs start new businesses every year. Over time, the new companies that grew and became successful would eventually hire a lawyer or two, occasionally use a law firm, and so on. Unfortunately, this approach would take years to have any discernible impact on demand and would be a lot harder to implement than simply reducing law school enrollments and/or tuition.

PART TWO

Building Things

5

—

Building Things Is Really Hard

It's conventional wisdom that entrepreneurship is what is going to drive our continued national competitiveness. We need new businesses, innovation, and new jobs. We hear it from politicians and journalists at every turn.

I've visited campuses around the country and know that droves of students are interested in startups. Many young people are attracted to the idea of entrepreneurship as a potential career path.

But most people will not actually go off and start their own company. And with good reason. Building things is very, very hard.

I know this from experience. In January 2000, five months after starting at Davis Polk and Wardwell, I left to cofound Stargiving.com, a site that helped celebrities raise money for their favorite charities. I hatched this plan with Jon Phillips, another attorney at the firm.

The concept behind Stargiving.com was that celebrities would donate their time for charity ("Play one-on-one with Magic Johnson!"). Sponsors would donate twenty-five cents on behalf of each person who clicked on the celebrity's charity event, and the visitor would see the sponsor's logo. Then, one of the people who clicked on the event would meet the celebrity. This model was based on the Hunger Site (now freerice.com), which became hugely popular back in 1999.

We thought we'd revolutionize fund-raising. Celebrities were already donating meet and greets at charity events. This way, a million people could have the chance to win. The event would raise a lot more money too, because sponsors would want the chance to be affiliated with the celebrity and the cause and would be seen with each micro-donation. Last, individuals would have the chance to do a good deed, raise money at no cost, and potentially meet a celebrity by spending just a few seconds of their time. Everybody wins. It was genius.

We faced a few small problems—we didn't have any money. We didn't know how to build a website (a very arcane process back in 2000). And we didn't know any celebrities.

Before quitting Davis Polk and Wardwell, I took a week off and tried to work on the business. I had several interesting meetings and made a rough draft of an investor presentation. It felt enough like progress that I gave notice the following week.

In retrospect, this was somewhat rash. But I figured there wasn't a better time to do it. It would only get harder, not easier, to quit. And I didn't have a mortgage or kids—I didn't even have a girlfriend. When else was I going to take a risk? Besides, I began thinking that the more daunting risk was waking up a decade later, wondering why I'd never done anything.

The first and most immediate step was to get money. I'd saved $10,000 from my time at the firm. My educational loans were about $1,200 a month, on top of my rent of $1,600 a month for a studio apartment. I figured I had three months to raise some cash. Given the myriad stories of dot-com success circulating at the time, it seemed like money was flowing freely. We adopted a valuation of $2 million and were trying to raise $20,000 for 1 percent of the company. Those were the days. I asked my friends to introduce me to anyone they knew who had an extra $20,000 sloshing around. I took my PowerPoint presentation to people's living rooms, boats, and offices—wherever anyone would have me. If I found myself alone in an elevator with someone, I'd start a conversation hoping it might lead somewhere.

Five months later, we had yet to raise a dime. It turns out people don't meet a twenty-five-year-old former corporate attorney trying to start a dot-com business and throw money at him. Most prospective investors were pretty kind, partially because I was in their house and knew someone who knew them. They'd say things like, "This is really exciting. Let me think it over and get back to you." But no checks came. Pretty soon I'd run through my savings and was living on my credit card. I moved out of my apartment and in with a friend.

It was incredibly discouraging; it was harder than anything I'd ever done before. But it also felt genuine. Before this, I'd thought that there were just two inputs for success—smarts and hard work. I began learning that accessing people resources and the world at large was its own separate dimension. I started adapting to my new role and circumstances. I was driven by the thought that Stargiving would eventually turn into a successful company, and once it did it would do a lot of good for various causes and create a lot of value.

It was around July that we got our first investor. It was a friend's brother-in-law, who had just sold a company and was eager to invest in a new project. He put up $25,000. I got the sense that he and his wife invested more because they liked me and wanted to be encouraging than because of any confidence that they'd get a financial return. I remember taking the check and running to the bank to cash it before they changed their minds. After that first check cleared, we generated a bit of momentum. We got another $25,000, followed by another. The biggest investment was from a friend of a friend who joined me at the company. We raised about $200,000 that summer. We also got an investment from Vanguarde Media, whose chief operating officer I met through a contact. Vanguarde helped us build the website. I started paying myself a salary of $48,000 or so to keep the lights on.

Another big break came when we met Beth Leonard, a former VH1 talent booker and wife of Darius Rucker, then the lead singer of the band Hootie and the Blowfish. Beth became our celebrity liaison, and through her and a few other connections we had generated after months of networking we were set to launch with Hootie and the Blowfish, Nikki Taylor, Magic Johnson, the MTV Video Music Awards, Muhammad Ali, Dan Patrick, an NBA locker room visit, and Edwin McCain events. We even got Anheuser Busch to sponsor several of the events, thanks to Beth.

During this period I had some unlikely and quite surreal experiences. There were a number of times when I thought to myself, how the heck am I sitting here having this meeting? I met Don Casey, then the head coach of the New Jersey Nets. Don took a shine to me and invited me to a game. I found myself courtside for a Nets game and left the building via the players' exit after the game. There were fans standing all around waiting for autographs. You should have seen how confused and silent they were when I came out right after Stephon Marbury.*

Later that year, I had a morning meeting with Brett Ratner (director of *X-Men: The Last Stand*, *The Family Man*, and the Rush Hour series) at his Hollywood mansion. Brett had a fully functioning nightclub on the lower level of his house, in which he had hosted a party for the Los Angeles Lakers the night before. There were stray photos of the party lying around, which included shots of Shaquille O'Neal, Rick Fox, and various models and actresses. It was like glimpsing an episode of *Entourage* before there was *Entourage*.

In retrospect, the only reason we got any attention or money was because the era was still pretty forgiving and the tech bubble hadn't burst yet. In that sense our timing was good.

Having raised some money, built a site, and booked some celebrities, we went live in October 2000 and got some tremendous press. I wound up on a CNN financial news program with Darius Rucker, talking about how we were going to revolutionize celebrity giving. We were written up in the *New York Times*, *USA Today*, on Yahoo!, and in other mainstream outlets. The day before the *Times* article hit, I went to sleep thinking, "Wow, tomorrow we're going to get thousands of visitors, and things will never be the same."

---

*On a personal note, I'm a very big NBA fan, so I quite enjoyed this.

The thousands turned out to be dozens. Much to my surprise, people don't read a newspaper, put it down, and then go seek out a website. Even worse, for those who did bother to check it out, the site was pretty boring. Visitors would click on a button with Darius's face on it, read about his cause, see Anheuser Busch make a donation on their behalf, and think, "Huh. That's interesting." Then they'd never come back. We found ourselves looking for ways to boost traffic to a pretty dull site that was not taking off like the wildfire we'd hoped.

In the next several months our situation became increasingly dire. The air had gone out of the tech bubble in a hurry. The NASDAQ went from 4,696 in February 2000 to 1,840 in March 2001. Mainstream stock investments lost more than 60 percent of their value as public companies like Yahoo!, Amazon, AOL, and others experienced massive stock price corrections.

The repercussions in New York City were stark and immediate. Companies that had been the darlings of the Silicon Alley tech press only months earlier (Flooz, Kozmo, Space.com, iWon, govWorks, and others[*]) began to struggle to stay afloat. Most were reliant upon continued investor financing and weren't producing meaningful revenue relative to their expenses. It was as if a giant hand had swept through Manhattan and started swatting companies away right and left.

We went out with the tide. Our website traffic was negligible, and Anheuser Busch's $5,000 sponsorship didn't take us very far. Reporters lost interest, as they were busy excoriating all dot-coms as money-losing flim-flams (or, in some cases, losing their jobs themselves). Our investors had no interest in continuing to

---

[*] The West Coast equivalents of the day were Pets.com, Webvan.com, and eToys.com, among others.

press forward; quite the opposite, they were hoping to get out what little money we had left of their investment. There weren't many alternatives. By the spring of 2001 the writing was on the wall. We were going to have to shut Stargiving down.

Entrepreneurship is about creativity. Entrepreneurs can move mountains individually. Entrepreneurs are born different.

None of these is correct.

There is a common and persistent belief out there that entrepreneurship is about creativity, that it's about having a great idea. But it's not, really. Entrepreneurship isn't about creativity. It's about organization building—which, in turn, is about people.

I sometimes compare starting a business to having a child. You have a moment of profound inspiration, followed by months of thankless hard work and waking up in the middle of the night.* People focus way too much on the inspiration, but, like conception, having a good idea isn't much of an accomplishment. You need the action and follow-through, which involves the right people, know-how, money, resources, and years of hard work.

I learned this the hard way. Here's a list of things you can reasonably do on the side as you're working a full-time job to explore an idea for a great new business:

1. Research your idea (figure out the market, talk to prospective customers about what they would like, see who your competitors are, and so forth).

---

*I can now talk about this from experience, as I had a baby boy, Christopher, in late 2012. I got married somewhere in the interim too.

2. Undertake legal incorporation and trademark protection (the latter when necessary; most companies don't need a trademark at first).

3. Claim a web URL and build a website or have it built; get company e-mail accounts.

4. Get a bank account and credit card (you'll generally have to use personal credit at first).

5. Initiate a Facebook page, a blog, and a Twitter account if appropriate.

6. Develop branding (e.g., get a logo designed, print business cards).

7. Talk it up to your network; try to find interested parties as cofounders, staff, investors, and advisers.

8. Build financial projections and draft a business plan (if necessary).

9. Engage in personal financial planning (e.g., cut back on expenses, budget for startup costs, and so on.)

10. Create a mock prototype and presentation for potential investors or customers.

If all of this sounds like a lot of work to do before you've even really gotten started, you're right. Getting this stuff done while holding down a job would be a significant commitment. You might not have time to hang out with friends and family and do the things people like to do when they're not at work. It is doable, though; I've seen it done or done it myself.

You're just getting started. There's a big jump in difficulty when it comes to the next things:

1. Raise money. In my experience, fledgling entrepreneurs focus way too much on the money—you can get most things done and figure out a lot without spending much. That said, most businesses require money to launch and get off the ground. For example, the average restaurant costs about $275,000 in construction and startup costs.[1] Finding initial funds is the primary barrier most entrepreneurs face. Many people don't have three or six months' worth of savings to free themselves up to do months of unpaid legwork.

2. Develop the product. Product development is a significant endeavor. Even if you're hiring someone to build your product, managing them to specifications is a huge task in itself. You can expect vendors to take twice as long and cost twice as much as you've planned for. Think of the last home improvement project you paid a contractor for; most experiences are like that. Depending on the product, you may need to travel to find the right ingredients, partners, and suppliers. This phase might require raising additional money as well. In some cases, you might want to patent your product, which will involve a patent search and thousands of dollars in patent attorney fees.[*]

3. Build a team. Most people don't build a business alone, and finding quality partners or employees can be time-consuming and unpredictable. Your first employee is going to look to you for guidance, and her productivity is going to depend on your ability to guide and manage. And with partners, you'll need to make sure you can work well with them, since they're going to be with you from the ground up and for years afterward.

---

[*]Patent attorneys are among the most highly specialized and expensive lawyers. The job requires both a law degree and a science background.

4. Get customers. Going to trade shows or trying to get your first handful of paying customers is typically a major time investment. This can involve web marketing, producing content, and search engine optimization, all of which take significant energy and resources to generate a return. Despite the advent of social media, most things gain traction and spread at a deliberate pace. Even if someone likes your service, it's not going to be a priority for him to go around telling friends about it or liking your service on Facebook. Think about your own behavior; when's the last time you went around telling everyone you know about a company you liked? Getting early sales is very hard work. You'll likely depend on relationships to help you get the ball rolling.

You could give most people a fantastic business idea, and they would get excited about it but wouldn't quit their job to take it on. And no one has an extra ten people in the back room waiting for a good idea either. How many great ideas have you had through the years that have remained just that thing you dreamed up with your friends that one time?

Starting a new business is generally going to be a multi-year commitment at the very least. One of my mentors, Manu Capoor of MMF Systems, once told me that it takes at least four or five years to see if a company is going to work. If you're exceptional, you can tell where you're going by year three. My experience has shown me that in almost every case, he was right.

If you just read business articles and blogs, you'll get the sense that tons of companies enjoy immediate success, particularly in the Internet realm. But those are the anomalies. For most, overnight success is an extreme rarity. Generally, a company makes progress incrementally. Someone (or multiple people) likely suffered while figuring out how to make it work. Even for the rare product or software application that does become a rapid hit, it often took the programmers, product developers, or designers time to build up the necessary expertise. They might have worked on some earlier product that no one ever heard of, learned from it, and come back to build something great. This is a good description of Rovio, which was around for six years and underwent layoffs before the "instant" success of the Angry Birds video game franchise. In the case of the Five Guys restaurant chain, the founders spent fifteen years tweaking their original handful of restaurants in Virginia, finding the right bun bakery, the right number of times to shake the french fries before serving, how best to assemble a burger, and where to source their potatoes before expanding nationwide.

Most businesses require a complex network of relationships to function, and these relationships take time to build. In many instances you have to be around for a few years to receive consistent recognition. It takes time to develop connections with investors, suppliers, and vendors. And it takes time for staff and founders to gain effectiveness in their roles and become a strong team.*

---

*Experienced entrepreneurs have a number of advantages where pace is concerned. First, they know roughly how long it will take to get something done if they've done it before. Second, they can move faster, because many of the necessary relationships are already in place (e.g., they can call people they've worked with, use the same lawyer, accountant, and public relations firm, draw on earlier investors, and reach out to past customers). Third, they can proceed more decisively because of greater confidence in their judgment, both internally and externally. Last, they sometimes have lots of money. These are all reasons why some entrepreneurs seem so prolific.

So, yes, the bar is high when you want to start a company. You'll have the chance to work on something you own and care about from day to day. You'll be 100 percent engaged and motivated, and doing something you believe in. You can lead an integrated life, as opposed to a compartmentalized one in which you play a role in an office and then try to forget about it when you get home. You can define an organization, not the other way around.

But even if you quit your job, hunker down for years, work hard for uncertain reward, and ask everyone you know for help, there's still a great chance that your new business will not succeed. Over 50 percent of companies fail within their first three years.[2] There's a quote I like from an unknown source: "Entrepreneurship is living a few years of your life like most people won't, so that you can spend the rest of your life like most people can't." Even this concept assumes a degree of success that may or may not come. Imagine spending years working on a business, putting your all into it, getting money from your friends and family, and telling everyone you know that you're building this new thing, only to have it flop. I've experienced this, and it's not easy to go through. Dave McClure of PayPal and 500 Startups has said of his own experience, "It was a hell of a lot of work for not a hell of a lot of return. And there are days when you sit in a corner and cry. You can't really do anything else. You don't have a social life. You don't really want to interact with family and friends because there's just not much context for them. Your world revolves around your startup and it's all about trying to survive and not look like an idiot in front of employees."[3]

This is the sort of challenge we want people to take on, despite the obstacles and likelihood of failure. People portray entrepreneurship as somehow glamorous or lucrative, which of course it can be after a while. But for most, it's an anonymous, stressful, isolating endeavor. Most of the work you do for your company is unglamorous, even gritty. And it's certainly not the optimal risk-adjusted way to maximize your bank account in most situations.

So why does anyone ever do it? Some entrepreneurs are not very good joiners. They struggle to find roles they're excited about in existing companies and thus feel prompted to start their own. Some just want to do their own things. But in the best of situations, entrepreneurs are motivated by solving problems. They clearly see that the world is missing what they have in mind to offer, and they can't rest until the world has their cookie, iPod, suitcase, software, or website in its hands. They then encounter ten thousand little problems on the way to solving the big problem they have in mind. They address these issues one by one and get others to help them. Over time, solving problems and building an organization that does so become addictive and second nature. It's less about creativity and intellect, and more about will, determination, and the willingness to take on the multitude of micro-issues in service of the big goal.

In most cases, it takes more than one person to overcome these thousands of little problems; it takes an organization. That's how entrepreneurship becomes about teams as much as it is about the individual founder(s). The more experienced an entrepreneur is, the more she tends to value working with stellar people and being part of a quality team from day one.

In most organizations, the top people are not just incrementally more productive than average workers; they're *much* more productive. Facebook founder Mark Zuckerberg was once quoted as saying the top programmer is one hundred times more productive than the average programmer. While that's a bit dramatic, it's true that having a handful of top-notch people on board early makes any company much more likely to establish itself and succeed. Devising a new and innovative product or delivering a new service is a lot more achievable if you have a few of the right people around.

As a startup progresses, people's roles often morph and grow over time. Ideally you're hiring someone not to do a job but to do or invent a bigger job when the company expands. At my last company we hired a brilliant guy, Mike Dinerstein, straight out of college to the marketing department. Over time, he realized that we needed to bulk up our online presence. He wound up teaching himself several programming languages and revamped much of our site, and over the next couple of years became the manager of a brand-new online marketing department that was built around him. He later returned to school to get his master's degree in computer science, something he hadn't even studied as an undergrad. Not coincidentally, the company's revenue went up dramatically while Mike was coming into his own. You're not always sure what your needs are going to be as the company grows; the right people will help you figure them out and fill whatever needs arise.

If you have strong early hires, it's highly attractive to other talented and hardworking people. There's an aphorism that A people hire A's, B people hire C's, and C people hire losers. The challenge is to hire A's from the outset and keep the quality high for as long as you possibly can. It's a million times easier to build a winning team if the first few players are talent magnets. On the flip side, it's brutal trying to pull together the right people if you have someone around early on who doesn't generate a high degree of confidence, enthusiasm, and respect. Cultures get built from the beginning, and whoever joins a company takes cues from whoever's already there.

When building a team, a common saying in the startup world is, "Slow to hire, fast to fire." Good organizations work very hard at recruiting and retaining the right people for every task—for production, sales and marketing, operations, customer service, finance, administration, and so on. Getting high-caliber people in place can mean the difference between a company failing or going on to hire thousands of employees. To paraphrase Margaret Mead, don't doubt what a small group of smart, committed people can accomplish—because that's the way everything starts.

Most entrepreneurs will tell you that the team around them makes all the difference in the world. If every promising growth company in the country had a cadre of top people trying to join it each year, we'd see dramatic results pretty quickly.

Finally, there's a notion that entrepreneurs are somehow innately talented or born that way. They just carve out their own path. The fact is that most people are capable of a range of activities depending upon need, environment, and how those people are developed.

Entrepreneurship is a process. You get better over time. The image of the college dropout entrepreneur who starts a world-class company is misleading. People like Bill Gates, Steve Jobs, and Mark Zuckerberg are highly visible outliers. Most twenty- to twenty-two-year-olds don't have the wherewithal to start or run a successful business at that young age, and this should be unsurprising, given that a majority of businesses fail within the first several years, regardless of the age of the founder. Most successful entrepreneurs failed once or twice when they were young. Before founding Microsoft, Bill Gates cofounded a company called Traf-O-Data that lost thousands of dollars and shut down.[4] Billionaire entrepreneur Mark Cuban recalls "coming home and having the lights turned off because [I] couldn't afford to pay the bills" when he was starting out.[5] Sam Walton's first Arkansas store went under before he started Walmart, and Henry Ford's first car company went out of business.

Entrepreneurs are themselves forged through experience. You wouldn't expect a doctor or athlete to be the best in his or her first several years, either. The key is to get the failures and lessons in as soon as possible so that you can learn from them, get up, and recover.

What sort of experience would you suggest to a twenty-two-year-old who wanted to start or run a business someday? You could ask him or her to start a company and learn the hard way. But this would be a bridge too far, and an extraordinarily costly endeavor. A better alternative would be to send him or her to work at a startup, working alongside a more experienced entrepreneur.

6

—

How You Get Better

I was twenty-six when Stargiving shut down. I lay on my floor, looking up at the ceiling, wondering how it had come to this. I still owed $100,000 in law school debt. I'd just been responsible for investor losses of hundreds of thousands of dollars and would be naturally lumped in with the second-rate dot-com entrepreneurs of the bubble who were now considered lousy businesspeople. My parents were concerned. The subtext of their questions to me was, *Didn't you used to be smart?*

It's hard to feel good after such a conspicuous failure. You feel bad for investors and your teammates. At my most cash-strapped, I started doing things like showering at my gym to use the free toiletries and going to Cosi to scarf down their free bread samples. But eventually you pick yourself up. You realize that no one died. Everyone will find other things to do, including you. Your family still loves you, your friends still like you, and women don't know you have a net worth of negative $100,000 unless you tell them.

I needed a job, and I had no desire to return to being a

lawyer. The past months had been a heady ride of trying to build a new organization from the ground up; there had been numerous highs and lows. I felt like I'd bitten from the proverbial apple and I couldn't forget what I'd seen. Though startup work was difficult, I believed I'd learned something and could get better.

I realized that in order to move forward, I needed to become a better businessperson. I decided to try to apprentice myself to a more experienced entrepreneur whom I would hopefully learn from.

I put the word out among my friends, and one of them came through, introducing me to three entrepreneurial wireless telecom executives who were starting a new company, Crisp Wireless. We got along immediately, and they needed someone to prepare their documentation. I became their vice president of business and legal development in return for a $60,000 salary and a couple of percentage points of equity in the company that vested over the next several years.

In the wake of the dot-com crash, there were troubled enterprises everywhere. Crisp gathered together assets, primarily a team of programmers that specialized in mobile software development. The programmers had prior clients in the form of Sony Music and Nextel Wireless. Crisp had designs on creating white-label mobile brands for big companies.

But these were tough times. Business was sparse, and the money the executives put in didn't last long. One day I came into the office and found that one of our salespeople had moved into the conference room because he couldn't pay his rent. His bedding was on the floor, and he took his shower in the office bathroom in the back. His luggage was lined up against a wall. (I told him, "You're living the dream!" He glared at me.) Before long I thought I might be in the same boat. By the spring of 2002, I'd stopped receiving any salary and was back to living on credit cards.

I figured it was time to leave Crisp.* Another friend reintroduced me to Manu Capoor, whom I'd met while I was networking for Stargiving. Manu was a former doctor and investment banker who had started a health care software company, MMF Systems, which aggregated paper patient data and made it available online. It seemed like a good product, one that made a positive difference. Manu had converted the company from business-to-consumer to business-to-business and wanted me to become the guy who talked to and trained the staff at hospitals and surgery centers.

I joined MMF in 2002 as vice president. We had no revenue in the new business, and a million or so in the bank that Manu had raised. I was at it again. I was getting paid around $65,000 plus some equity that vested over four years. My job was to get hospital nurses, administrators, clerks, doctors' office managers, surgeons, medical residents, and anesthesiologists to use and love our product. I was a combination trainer, salesperson, and client services relationship manager. Our first big client was Columbia Presbyterian Medical Center in New York City. I spent six months there, roaming the halls, befriending and training staff and doctors, and troubleshooting any issues that arose. After the trial period, the hospital signed a six-figure contract with MMF to manage its paper-based patient information. We expanded from

*The original partners who brought me in left, but Crisp Wireless went on to become a successful company years later thanks to a couple of key executives who stuck with it, especially Mary Park.

there to New York Presbyterian/Weill Cornell Medical Center, Montefiore Medical Center in the Bronx, the University of Medicine and Dentistry of New Jersey in Newark, and other regional hospitals.

Around the same time, as a side gig I rounded up some partners and began throwing parties on weekends under the name Ignition NYC. There were a couple of things that had inspired this idea. First, I'd read a book on the US Military Academy at West Point that described how cadets both led and followed someone different each year to develop as leaders.* I took that to mean that I should try to run something even while trying to learn from Manu. I wanted to prove to myself that I could build a business that made money.

Also, I was trying to be cool, and after accounting for loans and rent, I didn't have that much disposable income. Throwing parties enabled me to play host and meet people while actually making money instead of spending it. My partners were Amy Engelhardt, a woman that every guy I knew at the time had a crush on, and Gunny Scarfo, a developer who built our party network's website and database. For each party we got a pile of free drink tickets to use as we saw fit, plus a commission on revenue if we exceeded the establishment's expectations, which we did regularly. We had a few really big hits, including a fashion show at Lotus, a hot club at the time, and a 2004 New Year's Eve party on Madison Avenue that attracted over four hundred people and netted us thousands of dollars.†

---

*For a great read, see David Lipsky, *Absolutely American: Four Years at West Point* (New York: Vintage, 2004).

†New Year's Eve is the only time in the party business you can get away with charging people an arm and a leg and no one will care.

I learned a lot from the party business—it's great training for running a business in general. Among the lessons I learned:

- The default number of attendees is zero. You get out what you put in.
- The personal touch is always best. If you write or call people individually they'll come.
- Don't throw parties on Mondays or Tuesdays.
- Choose your partners wisely.
- The best way to get others to come to your party is to go to their parties. Reciprocity rules.*
- It's way easier to invite someone to a party and get them to come than it is to get a date with them.
- Don't save free drink tickets until the end of the night. Use them as soon as possible.
- Nothing makes someone happier than skipping a line.
- If a party gets too crowded, some people will leave.
- When presented with an opportunity to be a jerk or let it go, let it go.
- People get irrationally possessive and touchy about free gift bags.
- If no one has shown up in the first hour, don't worry—they'll show.

I got a great education and had some amazing times. If you want to throw a big party, give this a try—find a few people you like and respect but that you're not that close

---

*Plus, if you go to another party, you'll likely meet some people whom you'll want to invite to yours.

friends with—people who have networks that are different from the ones you have. Convince them to cohost a party with you. If that works, you'll be off to the races.

I worked for Manu and MMF from 2002 to 2005, and I learned a lot from him. He's a visionary and an incredible salesperson; MMF went on to raise a total of over $5 million. My client-facing team grew to eight people. The company went from essentially zero in annual revenue to more than $2 million during the time I was there.

Manu taught me that there are three ways to get things done in business: people, processes, and technology. He would say, "We're not building a consultancy, we're building a product business." He was always pushing to figure out what we were doing and to process and automate it. At first I didn't really understand where he was going, but I grew to appreciate it.

Many businesses start by having several talented people working on something. If they're very capable, they can build a business based on ingenuity and provide a service that someone will pay for. In our case, we had some smart types around who could drop in on a hospital and improve the information flow by figuring out the bottlenecks (in conjunction with our online offerings).

Eventually, if you're smart you identify what the consistent issues are and recognize patterns. You become able to process things in a replicable way. At this stage, it's possible that someone who's not quite as experienced, talented, or creative can do some of the work, because you've figured out what needs to be done. In our case, we realized that one of the steps was behavior management and education in physicians' offices. We hired people who would go to these offices and interact with the secretaries who were sending documents to the hospital. Generally speaking, the more process-driven a job is, the less vital the nature of the person you're hiring for it.

If a task has been processed very carefully, it's sometimes possible to automate it. You can have technology perform a task instead of a worker. For example, we could have an automated e-mail reminder notifying physicians' offices that they hadn't submitted insurance information to the hospital instead of having someone call or visit them. When you get to this point, you're at the product level and the business becomes predictable and scalable. This is what we were going for, because then our software could be more quickly rolled out to a larger number of hospitals.

This is the progression many startups tackle. They begin with talented people who are trying to solve a problem, and there are many twists and turns. Eventually, they figure out a solution to the point where they hire people for more defined roles and grow their business. Finally, they automate as much as they can to reach the product stage, if that's feasible (it's often not feasible for "service" businesses or consultancies; these businesses thus retain an emphasis on hiring people who can maintain the quality of the service being offered).

Being part of this process helped my perspective a lot. But by my fourth year at MMF I began to seek a new environment. I'd spent four years in urban hospitals, and after a while they felt kind of redundant. I started looking for a change. I was forthright about this with Manu; he said he would be sorry to see me go, but as a fellow entrepreneur he understood.

Around this time a friend, Zeke Vanderhoek, approached

me about becoming the new head of his test-prep company, Manhattan GMAT. Zeke had started the business as a solo tutor in 2000, and a year later a mutual friend introduced us to each other. He initially asked me to write drills and curricular material for the new company. Eventually, I began teaching classes and making presentations as the company grew, due to Zeke's indefatigability and his immense talents as a teacher. I taught and pinch-hit for Manhattan GMAT part-time throughout its first several years and was the company's first instructor.*

Zeke's ambition was to start a charter school in Washington Heights, a New York City neighborhood where he had been a teacher for Teach for America. He was looking for a new CEO to replace him and thought that I'd be the perfect fit, in large part because we'd worked together so he had a sense of how I operated. I'd been helping the company part-time for years—the best way to get comfortable with someone is to work with him or her. Zeke and I came to terms; I would spend some time learning the business and would then become the CEO. Manhattan GMAT was still a small business with only five staffers, and there wasn't a lot of cash flow—I was to be paid $65,000 initially. But as CEO I'd get some equity. And I was set to run a business again, about five years after the failure of Stargiving.

Someone reading this is probably thinking, "Wait a minute, didn't this guy make six figures as a lawyer? Why does he keep taking these jobs that are paying him half that? Couldn't he

---

* I'd taken the GMAT in order to have a quantitative credential and gotten a 780. I'd been a teaching assistant in law school and an LSAT instructor, so I had ample experience as a teacher.

have just gone back to a firm and gotten his old job back?" Of course I would have liked to have been paid more money— who wouldn't? Many of my friends and classmates were making a lot of money at this point, and New York is an expensive place to live. But I wanted to find a startup that I could have an impact on, and it didn't seem realistic to show up and say "I want $125k because I once got paid that as a lawyer" unless it was clear I was delivering that much value.

To me, different roles in different organizations presented completely different levels of engagement. On one end is being the CEO of your own company or working for a small company. You're charged up and feel like your success or failure relies on how much you bring to the table each day. On the other end is working for a big professional services firm for a client that you have very little personal investment in. I wanted to care about what I was doing from day to day and to feel like I was potentially making a difference in building a business.

This was a shift from when I'd graduated from college years earlier. At that time I had a very limited conception of jobs, careers, and what I wanted to do. Basically, my thinking in a nutshell was to seek higher-paid 'intellectual' work. This proved unhelpful when I didn't enjoy being a corporate lawyer at all. After starting a company and working at several other startups, I got a much better sense of what would make a job enjoyable for me. I started categorizing job attributes that were important to me.[*]

I wanted a position that required broad management in

---

[*] The list of job traits I came up with is in appendix D; some people have found them helpful.

a growth enterprise that was doing something I could get excited about. I wanted to be an owner and to be committed to helping a team achieve its goals. Money would be great, but I was happy to be paid based on the value I was bringing to an enterprise, which presumably would be reflected in its success (or failure). The culture of the environment was important to me too. Basically, I wanted to build something.

I knew that these factors applied only to those fortunate enough to have significant choices as to what sort of employment they take; most people take what they can get. That said, I figured I was still relatively young and could afford to take some risks and push myself in the direction I wanted to go. I could always declare penance later. By the time I arrived at Manhattan GMAT, I was charged up and ready to make a mark.

7

Running a Company

I was thirty when I started running Manhattan GMAT, and I was pumped. The company had a lot going for it, and I was looking to build on and preserve its strengths while also making the organization better equipped for the next phase of development.

The first thing I did was absorb as much as I could from Zeke. He'd built the company from the ground up. Zeke was single-minded about the role of the instructor and about product quality. He often turned down expansion opportunities if he thought it would compromise quality in any way. Thanks to him, the foundation of the company was rock solid.

After reflecting on what made the company distinct, I articulated three core values and started putting them up on a screen before each meeting:

- Help students achieve their goals
- Our standard is excellence
- Build a strong team

I hoped these principles would help guide and influence our thinking and decision making.

We put up a big whiteboard in the office to start openly displaying various company-wide metrics, including the number of students in each market, monthly revenues, and year-over-year growth. We conducted regular company-wide reviews of student surveys to ensure that our satisfaction scores remained the best in the industry (an average of over 4.6 out of 5 overall, almost universal recommendation rates) and followed up on issues in real time.

One of my beliefs was that the lifetime value of each student was based on his satisfaction level and how many friends he told about the company afterward. We focused on delivering the best educational experience and results we could, which in my mind meant having the happiest and most dedicated and motivated teachers and staff.

Our instructors were getting paid $100 per hour to teach or tutor—three to four times the market rate—so they tended to be pretty happy. Still, having been an instructor myself, I knew that it was easy to feel somewhat divorced from the company as a whole. I started regularly informing instructors how the company was performing and flew those based in other cities to New York once or twice a year for gatherings and parties (nerdily called "convocations"). We also built on instructor input and feedback to continuously improve the curriculum, and we gave cash bonuses for good suggestions and hired a number of instructors to develop materials or products in addition to teaching.

For the full-time staff, it was important to me that they regard our little test-prep company as a great place to build a career. I decided to invest in our corporate culture.* We had regular staff outings to celebrate record months. The company would pay for lunch as long as you ate with someone different each week. Each June, I had the whole company over to my one-bedroom apartment for a party. The company bought cheap season tickets to one team's games each year (the Knicks, Mets, or Yankees). We had an annual weekend retreat where we chartered a bus and rented a big place in the Hamptons, at the Jersey Shore, or in Killington, Vermont, for a couple of nights. Some of these things cost the company money. They probably shaved our profit margins by a percent or two each year. But I figured that if these expenses kept turnover low and morale high, they would pay off many times over in high performance and consistent growth. We had a nucleus of dedicated and talented team members, and I wanted to keep them and their teams as satisfied and committed as possible.

Chris Ryan was the first instructor who joined me as a full-time staffer. Chris graduated from Harvard with a physics degree in 1991, and, inspired by his brother's military service during the first Gulf War, joined Teach for America, then in only its second year of existence. After his stint with Teach for America in Long Beach, California, Chris continued to teach physics and chemistry in Greensboro, North Carolina. After teaching for years, Chris found he needed a change and applied to business school. After getting his MBA from Duke University, he became a management consultant at

---

*I'd read Jim Collins and Jerry Porras, *Built to Last: Successful Habits of Visionary Companies* (New York: HarperBusiness), and was strongly influenced by it.

McKinsey and Company in New York, serving various large corporate clients. He left McKinsey after a couple of years to become an independent movie producer, ferrying *Solo Dios Sabe*, starring Diego Luna, around the festival circuit. Needing a supplementary source of income while toiling as an indie film producer, Chris, armed with his 790 GMAT score, impeccable teaching background, and years as an amateur musician and performer, saw an advertisement to teach for Manhattan GMAT and started working for the company part-time in 2003.

I used to joke that Manhattan GMAT was like the woman you met at a bar—you might date her, but you didn't think you were going to marry her. My job was to convince people like Chris to invest their careers and full-time energies in the little test-prep company they'd taken as a transitory gig to pay the bills. When Chris agreed to join as the head of product and instructor development it was a great day for the company; he's the sort of person you could build a world-class organization with, and that was our goal.

"Build a strong team" guided much of what I did for the next five-plus years. A significant part of my job as CEO was to serve as the final interviewer for prospective instructors, which happened several times a week. Because we paid so much more than other test-prep companies, we had no shortage of people applying to teach for us, despite our stringent requirements. The prerequisites for instructor applicants included a 99th percentile score on an actual GMAT (760 or higher out of 800, 40 points higher than the average Harvard Business School graduate); and prior experience as a teacher. Of the people who satisfied these criteria, half did not make it past the phone interview and online teaching audition. The other half were flown to New York for a multi-hour teaching audition in front of me, Chris, and a third panelist (this person varied from interview to interview), during which we would give candidates hard problems they hadn't seen before to solve, prepare, and teach.

We wanted teachers who measured themselves by what usable skills their students were developing. The best teachers would start a particular lesson, ask a student a question, or poll the class to gauge where everyone's knowledge was, and continuously get new input to decide how to most effectively proceed. They could sense changes in energy level in the room and would adjust accordingly. They were infinitely adaptable and constantly assessing, building from the student up rather than the lesson down.

We also wanted to like them as human beings. After all, we were going to work with these people for years and trust them with our brand and livelihood. If we didn't like someone, chances were pretty good students wouldn't, either.

If this sounds like a high standard, it was. The instructors we gathered over the years were the best we could find, literally the best teachers in the country. When we found someone who had the abilities and attributes we were looking for, it was a great day. That instructor was going to do a phenomenal job teaching for the company, help hundreds of students achieve their goals, make good money in a job she would enjoy, and build our business for years to come.

Abby Pelcyger was an example of a winning candidate. Abby graduated from MIT and taught for Teach for America (TFA) in an underperforming school in Philadelphia. She got bitten by the teaching bug, and was a math teacher in Philadelphia when she applied to teach for us, years after her commitment to TFA had ended. Teaching at Manhattan GMAT enabled her to make an additional $30,000 by teaching six hours a week, which would be a huge supplement to a public schoolteacher's salary. As Abby put it, we allowed her to "support her teaching habit." Abby got rave reviews and became a star in Philly. Eventually we made her an instructor liaison who went to other cities during the summer to take instructors out for dinner and see what was on their minds.

One of our most memorable auditions was from Ron Purewal from San Francisco. Ron graduated first in his class from Stanford with a chemistry degree and scored a perfect 800 on the GMAT the weekend after he heard about us from another instructor. Ron casually asked us to name a famous document (we chose the Declaration of Independence), and he then proceeded to reproduce it from memory, writing the text upside down on a piece of paper facing us so that we could read it.

In Boston we had Dan Gonzalez, an engineering graduate from Dartmouth who had taught high school physics and was an accomplished musician. Also in Boston was Eric Caballero, a UCLA electrical engineering graduate who went on to get his MBA at MIT and was building a software company consulting practice. Eric was the first in his family to go to college, and he taught in a boisterous style that put students immediately at ease. In New York there was Gregg Lachow, the former editor of the *Harvard Lampoon* (he bossed around Conan O'Brien), who went on to direct more than a dozen independent films before settling in as a high-level teacher, and Jon Schneider, a painter and artist from Amherst College who wanted to supplement his creative endeavors and loved to teach.

Despite their talent and qualifications, most candidates we saw were not excellent teachers. Some were boring and did not naturally hold students' attention. Others didn't have a very strong grasp of the math or grammar underlying the test and, despite their ninety-ninth-percentile test scores, would have trouble explaining the material comprehensively. Still others weren't very likable. But the most common failing was that most of them weren't attuned to what was going on in their students' heads—they likened teaching to broadcasting or delivering content as opposed to skill building from the student up. We were looking for instructors who were student-centered and would never walk away from a classroom thinking "That was a great class" while students were left thinking "I need to go home and study what just happened." We passed on four out of five candidates who made it to the final round.

Meeting and interviewing all of these people affected my view of how the world worked in terms of talent finding a home. Here were dozens of brilliant academics, engineers, creative writers, freelance tutors and educators, women balancing parenting responsibilities, former bankers, management consultants and lawyers looking to start their own projects, entrepreneurs looking for a side income—all of them very gifted in various ways (having scored a ninety-ninth percentile on a test designed for college graduates), and almost all underutilized by the world at large. I'd heretofore imagined that the world was pretty good at finding and making use of people's capacities, particularly if people stood out. Yet here were hundreds of cases to the contrary.

This was confirmed and reinforced by my experiences with my classes of GMAT students. I taught dozens of classes, and hundreds of students, from 2002 through 2010. There were many very talented, hardworking, well-educated people in my classes. But for all of their efforts, they seldom felt at home professionally (probably one reason they were applying to business school). Our hundreds of GMAT students often seemed to be on a quest, searching for something that they were having trouble finding.

One student, whom I'll call Sam, was a very smart economics major from Princeton. She had worked in investment banking at Morgan Stanley in New York for two years and found that it wasn't the right fit for her. She decided that she would rather work in corporate strategy, and got an in-house job at the Walt Disney Company in Los Angeles. After a couple of years at Disney, she needed a change again, so she enrolled at Harvard Business School. She decided that she wanted to work in online education and needed product expertise, so she became a product manager at Zynga, the online social gaming company, in San Francisco. In my eyes, Sam's quest was emblematic of many of our students' experiences.

Still, business was good. From 2006 to 2009, Manhattan GMAT's revenues rose from about $3 million to well over $10 million. It was an excellent four years. Our employee count rose from six to thirty full-timers, with more than a hundred instructors and part-time staff. We expanded across the country to Philadelphia, Seattle, Austin, San Diego, Houston, Atlanta, Dallas, Ann Arbor, Salt Lake City, Phoenix, Denver, and Washington, DC, and internationally to Toronto, London, and Paris. We gained most of the top banks and consulting firms as corporate clients, including McKinsey and Company, the Boston Consulting Group, Goldman Sachs, Bank of America, Deloitte, JPMorgan Chase, Morgan Stanley, and many others. Our books were on sale at Barnes and Noble and Amazon, and we sold tens of thousands of copies every season. We eventually became number one in GMAT prep in the United States, serving more business school applicants than any other company. We expanded into the LSAT and the GRE to diversify as our market share grew.

During my first year on the job I met and started dating Evelyn, who would later become my wife. On our first date she talked about her ex-boyfriend the whole time. I somehow saw past this.* I don't think it's a coincidence that things clicked with Evelyn soon after I started working at Manhattan GMAT. If you're invested in your job and you like what you're doing, it's a lot easier to wind up in a quality relationship.

For me, running Manhattan Prep for five years and seeing the company grow and succeed shaped and changed my outlook. Much of it went against the grain of what I'd absorbed from my earlier experiences.

When Zeke had approached me with the opportunity back in 2005, I'd been a little bit hesitant. Part of it was that the test-prep business seemed like a niche. Hospitals and health care software represented an enormous market. With GMAT prep it would be a more confined playing field. It was a smaller pond.

I pretty quickly found that you didn't need to play in a billion-dollar market to be successful. If you're a company that reaches $10 million in revenue with 10 percent margins, that's $1 million a year to reinvest or distribute to shareholders. That's a lot for a small group of people, even after taxes.

As the company grew, it branched out into publishing, the

---

*For the guys reading this, Evelyn's really pretty.

LSAT, and the GRE, all of which grew to be successful. In 2008 we partnered with an admissions consulting firm. The ceiling kept getting higher and higher. I found that it's okay if your organization is in a well-defined market that doesn't stretch into the hundreds of millions.*

One reason that people and press gravitate toward huge markets is because venture capitalists require it. Investors need to see enormous market potential in order to conceivably get the home run (e.g., Twitter, Facebook) that will make their portfolio pay off.

Zeke was a more typical entrepreneur in that he never had venture capital.[1] Even more remarkably, he didn't have any angel investors or financing to speak of aside from credit cards. He built the business brick by brick, satisfied student by satisfied student. Even as the company grew to millions in revenue, we funded our growth out of revenue and reinvested whatever we made in the business. When people saw the operation in the later years, they would always ask, "How were you guys funded?" When I told them we were self-funded or "bootstrapped," they couldn't believe it.

Not taking money meant not answering to anyone but ourselves.

Prior to Manhattan Prep, I'd been accustomed to something of a venture capital mind-set from my time at Stargiv-

---

*It's easy to get fixated on companies with billion-dollar valuations in billion-dollar markets. Companies like Airbnb, Dropbox, Square, and the like are highly visible, but they operate in arenas in which there will probably be only one or two big winners and they're not the norm. You can still do very well as long as you do well within your space and figure out new ways to grow. If anything, the competition is likely to be a little bit more manageable in a niche than if you go into, say, search engines.

ing and MMF: you raise money, build momentum, and try to keep your investors excited. There is an element of storytelling and expectation management. Of course customers are important, but so are your investors.

With Manhattan Prep there were no investors to placate. We had the best possible source of revenue and feedback—our customers. We spent money only as we made it.

I found this made our decisions pure and unfettered. We could make commitments that would bear fruit six, twelve, or twenty-four months down the line (or might never do so), without worrying about what it would do to our numbers in the short term or how it would appear. If we liked instructors and they were contributing, we had liberty to compensate them in a way that made them feel appropriately valued. We continuously invested in our curriculum, even though it was a short-term drag every time we did it. We could spend money on better online tools and new products from which it would take months or even years to show any measurable return.

Looking back now, I realize how rare and fortunate this was. In most environments it's a constant struggle to align management toward the long-term interests of the business. Many startups have investors who will want their money back in a particular time frame (most investment funds have a cycle of five years). Any public company has the glare and scrutiny of quarterly earnings reports and analyst calls. If you can pull it off where ownership and management are 100 percent aligned for the long term, it's extraordinary and a big advantage.

This focus helped us thrive relative to our competitors.

Another company, Veritas Prep, launched at the same time as Manhattan GMAT, and with the same general idea. Veritas expanded quickly and had an early lead. It got tons of press; its founders were even on the cover of *Entrepreneur* magazine. In 2006 it was more than twice the size of Manhattan GMAT.

Our company eventually surpassed theirs through word of mouth. We did a better job helping students than they did. Students pay more attention to what their friends say than who's on the cover of what.

Many businesses enjoy a great deal of attention, enthusiasm, and even goodwill, and still don't succeed.* It's easy to get PR and success confused.

With Manhattan GMAT we kept our heads down and just tried to do our best work. The people who needed to know about us knew about us, and that's all that mattered. Again, building a company isn't about having the right idea; it's about who forms the better organization, one that can deliver day in and day out.

By my fifth year, we were teaching thousands of students in classrooms around the country and online. When I got advice from smart businesspeople or consultant types who looked at our business, they would generally point out a couple of things.

First, we were paying our instructors more than necessary. If we were paying $100 per hour and the market rate

---

*For example, Color was a much-hyped start-up in 2012 that raised $40 million and then almost immediately disappeared. People loved Twinkies, and everyone knows about them, yet Hostess went bankrupt. Meanwhile, Reyes Holdings is a multibillion-dollar private company you've never heard of. Attention and commercial success have an uncertain relationship.

was $20 to $50, why not drop it to $80 or $90? It's not like instructors could leave and go somewhere else.

Second, we were told we should increase our course prices. After all, we were paying our instructors more and we were a premium product. We had Goldman Sachs and McKinsey as clients. We should be charging more than the competition.

These suggestions were probably technically correct, particularly when we were only marginally profitable in the early years. But I always ignored them.

We believed it was our mission to get the best instructors in the country and make them feel like they had found a home. One hundred dollars per hour seemed like a rate only a highly paid professional would get. It made our instructors happy and proud. Our turnover was less than 10 percent per year and due mainly to major life changes (e.g., one instructor moved to Baton Rouge; another became a business school professor) in a field where the turnover tends to be as high as 100 percent per year. Even if we could potentially get our instructors to accept $95 an hour or whatever, that wasn't what we were about. We instead went the opposite direction and implemented a bonus pool so that instructors started getting a year-end bonus based on tenure in 2006. We created a high-level teacher culture that we believed would lead to a better and more uniform experience for students.

We also didn't want to be a test-prep company only for people who could pay an arm and a leg. We sold our books and online resources for as little as twenty dollars apiece. We had free downloadable flash cards on the site. We had to charge more for private tutoring given that our instructors got paid such a high rate, but I always wanted our courses to be at the market price so that students would feel they got the best value possible. We were growing, and it didn't seem necessary to raise prices.

I was proud anytime students came to us and wound up with the result they wanted after using other companies to no avail. I felt like we were introducing a correlation between work ethic and performance.

An organization should have some values beyond optimizing a set of numbers. The choices you make inform what those values are. You've got to stand for something.

Throughout these years of growth, various suitors called asking if the company might be for sale. Kaplan Test Prep called to invite me to a one-on-one lunch with its CEO, John Polstein, whom I liked a great deal. An executive from Princeton Review visited, and we had several private equity firms seek us out. In 2009, Zeke and I decided to entertain suitors, in large part because Zeke's charter school, the Equity Project, was in full swing.* It wasn't an easy decision, but we felt that having a well-resourced parent would ensure that the company would thrive in the long term. After a competitive bidding process, we agreed to be acquired by Kaplan and the Washington Post Company in December of that year.

I remember the day vividly. After all the documents were signed, I sat there and waited for the transfer to clear. I was

---

*Zeke's school, the Equity Project, is not an ordinary school. It was innovative, paying teachers $125,000 per year on the same budget as any other school by removing administrators and asking more of those teachers. Zeke believed that excellent teachers were the key driver of student success, and that paying them equitably was the way to attract and retain outstanding teachers. He had seen money flowing to everything but the teachers in his earlier schools and thus had built a new school to change that. The Equity Project and Zeke were featured on *60 Minutes*, and the Bill and Melinda Gates Foundation is now measuring results.

sitting at my web browser, hitting *refresh* over and over again until it cleared in the late afternoon. And there it was. I let out a "Yeah!" and emerged from my office. I walked around dispensing checks to employees, as we had set aside a bonus pool for both staff and instructors. It's a lot of fun giving away money. I was Asian Santa Claus for a day.

I went home for the holidays the following week. At this point my parents were quite pleased with me; my assuming the mortgage on their apartment likely had something to do with that. I zeroed out my student loans that week too. I'd gone from scrapping and scrimping for almost a decade to being a thirty-four-year-old millionaire.

8

Rent-Seeking versus Value Creation

Manhattan Prep started out as one lone tutor in a Starbucks coffee shop. Less than ten years later, it was a leading national education and publishing business that employed over one hundred people and was acquired by a public company for millions of dollars. How did that happen?

We delivered a service that customers liked more than what was otherwise available. They sought us out and rewarded us with their business. We hired more people, grew, and kept improving. This process—a new company filling a need and flourishing as a result—is an example of value creation. It's the fuel of economic growth, and what our country has been seeking a formula for. It's the process that leads to new businesses and jobs.

Value creation has a polar opposite: rent-seeking. In the 1980s, economists began noticing that countries with ample natural resources experienced lower economic growth rates than others. From 1965 to 1998 in the OPEC (oil-producing) countries, gross domestic product per capita decreased on average by 1.3 percent, while in the rest of the developed world, per capita growth increased by 2.2 percent (for an overall difference of 3.5 percent). This was a surprise—if you had lots of oil in the ground, wouldn't that give you more wealth to invest and thus spur more rapid growth?

Economists cited a number of factors to explain this "resource curse," including internal and external conflict, corruption, lower monitoring of government, lack of diversification, and being subject to higher price volatility.

One other possible explanation on offer was that a country's smart people will wind up going to work in whatever industry is throwing off money (like the oil industry in Saudi Arabia). Thus fewer talented people are innovating in other industries, dragging down the growth rate over time. This makes sense—it's a lot easier for a gifted Saudi to plug into the Ministry of Petroleum and Mineral Resources and extract economic value than to come up with a new business or industry.

Does this sort of thing happen in the United States? Yes, you can make money through rent-seeking as opposed to value or wealth creation. Take cybersquatters—it's perfectly legal to buy up thousands of domain names, sit on them, and charge hundreds or thousands of dollars or more when someone wants to start "diamond.com" (that name sold for $7.5 million in 2006), as long as you don't violate an existing company's trademark. There is no value generated despite the sometimes exorbitant prices and the money changing hands.* Other classic examples of rent-seeking include lobby-

---

* A cybersquatter asked for $10,000 for www.vfa.org when we were looking at domain names for Venture for America; we declined. For a list of top URL sales, see http://www.domaining.com/topsales/—it's a multimillion-dollar industry.

ing to be given a greater share of wealth or limiting access to lucrative occupations to stifle competition.

Most economic activities fall somewhere on a spectrum between pure value creation and rent-seeking. Let's say that you want to take your company public on the New York Stock Exchange. Only a handful of institutions handle major public offerings (Goldman Sachs, Morgan Stanley, JP Morgan Chase, Credit Suisse, Citi, Bank of America Merrill Lynch, Barclays, UBS, and a few others), and they often work together to market a new stock. So your choices are going to be pretty limited in terms of institutions and prices. At least one study showed that US initial public offering (IPO) fees were higher than their European counterparts because of fewer banks competing for the business.[1] Google tried to circumvent this structure back in 2004 by engaging in a "Dutch auction" (where bidders set the price of shares) for its IPO to make its shares more accessible and to lower fees. But no other major company has tried anything similar since, in part because Google had mixed results.[2] From March 2012 to March 2013, the eight firms listed above underwrote IPOs of over $37 billion in shares, collecting fees of over $2 billion themselves.[3]

Now, there's clearly immense value for a company that's looking to raise capital on the public markets—access to tens of millions of dollars in investment, typically. But at this stage only a handful of organizations have the necessary track records and relationships with institutional buyers to be able to plausibly handle a large stock offering. And for the company, it's a bit like getting married—you only do it once, and you want to do it right. It's a high-stakes process, and there's no repeating.[*] So it's not really the kind of situation in which a company's going to be fighting to choose the most inexpensive provider. The major banks have the IPO market pretty well in hand. This also illustrates how the finance industry is dependent upon innovation elsewhere for long-term growth.

If a really smart guy shows up at Credit Suisse's equity underwriting department, it's a little bit like the smart Saudi heading to the Ministry of Petroleum and Mineral Resources. There's an existing franchise that's going to throw off a lot of money in the coming years. If he can maneuver to be close to the geyser, he's going to get paid a lot regardless of whether the geyser works measurably better due to his being there. As we've seen, up to 25 percent of employed seniors from our top universities are heading to financial services each year. Our financial services industry (and to a lesser extent its attendant legal industry) plays an equivalent role to the oil industry in Saudi Arabia in terms of talent attraction.

You can see a similar dynamic at work in other fields with fixed slots. There were 682 orthopedic surgery residents in the United States in 2012. That number is set because there are only so many funded residency slots in teaching hospital programs throughout the country.[4] If I were to kick butt in medical school and get one of these residencies, I would be

---

[*] These features are one reason why, for example, real estate brokers' fees have remained stable. If you only have to do it once and the stakes are high, you'll pay the governing rate even in an era of freely available info. See Brad Stone, "Why Redfin, Zillow, and Trulia Haven't Killed Off Real Estate Brokers," *Bloomberg Businessweek*, http://www.businessweek.com/articles/2013-03-07/why-redfin-zillow-and-trulia-havent-killed-off-real-estate-brokers.

on the way to becoming an orthopedic surgeon, probably the most coveted residency due to money, lifestyle, low morbidity of patients, gratification from restoring mobility, and other factors.

But let's say that I didn't make it and fell short—there would still be 682 orthopedic surgeons five years from now because the next guy would have gotten that slot. We're all competing to fit through the same finite gate. The value difference if I perform really strongly and get one of these coveted spots is not one more surgeon—it's the gap between me and the 683rd person who didn't get it (and perhaps went into a less prestigious or less lucrative specialty).

From a value creation standpoint, it's not ideal for a massive level of talent to be going to existing enterprises that have captured large economic rents or where people are fighting for a set of finite slots. The rents and slots will stay essentially constant. Contrast this with new business formation. If I were to say, "There are only going to be 682 new successful businesses started in the United States next year," people would instantly regard that as ridiculous. It's unknown and unknowable. But we all know that if another enterprising team comes along and starts a cool company, that number goes up by one.

What does the world look like on the other end of the spectrum, where you're not rent-seeking or competing for spots? I met a very engaging young guy last year in Providence, named Walker Williams. Walker was a web designer in his teens and kept designing for startups while he was a student at Brown studying history. While he was still a student, he founded a company, Jobzle, to help businesses more easily and quickly post part-time jobs and internships. Building a two-sided market wasn't easy, though; Jobzle wound up powering a local nonprofit job board and never took off.

As Walker was graduating in 2011, his favorite campus dive bar shut down.[5] He and his friend, Evan Stites-Clayton, saw dozens of mourners on Facebook and Twitter and decided to see if they could create a T-shirt around the buzz. They called their local screen printer, only to find out that they had to pay for everything up front (thousands of dollars for two hundred or more T-shirts) and that they needed to know exactly how many T-shirts, and what sizes, would be needed. It would take two weeks for the shirts to be ready. It seemed like a nonstarter.

Instead of giving up, they threw together a website with a basic idea; if they could get at least two hundred people to reserve a shirt, then they would organize and coordinate the printing and ship directly to buyers. If they couldn't reach their goal, no one would get charged. It took them about five hours to code and build the page, e-mail it around, and post their plan on social media. Once it went out, over four hundred people ordered a T-shirt. Walker and Evan pocketed $2,000 in profit at five dollars per shirt. Other clubs, communities, and individuals reached out and wanted the same thing for their cause or event.

Walker and Evan knew they were onto something big. They had some relationships through Betaspring, a Providence-based startup accelerator. An angel investor loved the idea so much that he wrote a $200,000 check the same day they pitched him. They launched Teespring in 2012, complete with added functionality and products (sweatshirts). Over the next ten months they produced over two million dollars' worth of customized apparel and hired nine more people to keep up with growth. As the company's momentum grew, their investor, Bill Cesare, joined full-time as chief operating officer.

Teespring isn't that big a company yet. But think about the value already created in the first year or so—thousands of people with apparel they like helping people or causes they care about, hundreds of thousands of dollars raised by groups, individuals, and nonprofits, and twelve jobs in Providence and counting. If Bill's investment does well, he'll probably invest in another company with the gains. Just think, if Walker and Evan had never started Teespring, none of this would ever have happened. That's the essence of value creation.

This is not to say that the path into the frontier is easy. It's not. Walker worked at several other startups throughout his college years, most of which did not pan out. He was a veteran by the time he graduated from college, which is unusual. The point is that not all jobs are created equal. Walker has a job—as CEO and cofounder of Teespring—that's producing massive value and opportunities for others. He could have gotten a job as, say, a management consultant in Boston that paid him a higher starting salary. Walker would have plugged into a large preexisting value network and taken on a well-defined role. He might even have boxed someone else out because the consulting firm gave him the offer and not the next guy.

We're all better off because Walker is busy creating value. He's better off too. The question is, how do we get more people to take the harder road and do the same?

PART THREE

Solving the Problem

9

The Qualities We Need

A friend told me about a young Princeton graduate she knew named Cole. Cole studied mathematics and went to work for a hedge fund directly out of school. He's now making well into six figures at the age of twenty-four. That's his whole story to date.

That's success and the American way. And yet how excited are you about Cole's trajectory? Think about it for a second.

I'll admit that I'm not too psyched about it, even though I have friends at hedge funds who are very intelligent, stand-up guys and even philanthropists, and I know that hedge funds are positive in that they provide diversified investment opportunities to large pools of capital.

My lack of enthusiasm comes down to a few things. If Cole successfully analyzes an opportunity for the hedge fund and it invests slightly more effectively, that will be a win for the fund's managers and its investors. But there will very likely be an equivalent loss on the other side of the investment (whoever sold it to them makes out slightly less well for having undervalued the asset). It's not clear what the macroeconomic benefit is, unless you either favor the hedge fund's investors over others or have a very abstract view toward capital markets working efficiently.

Cole is almost certainly very smart. But what has he done to merit his almost immediately elevated stature in life? He's never hazarded anything. He hasn't demonstrated any outstanding character or virtue, unless you consider studying math and being really smart intrinsically virtuous. He's never had to go against the grain or go out on a limb. His rewards seem a little bit exaggerated for his accomplishments.

Finally, Cole's life is very quickly going to become quite different from that of the vast majority of humanity. His housing, education, and professional circles will take him into rarefied air. He'll donate to causes and he'll retain an intellectual interest in policy matters. But his experiences are going to be wildly divergent and probably make it tougher for him to understand others' customary everyday concerns and struggles over the coming years. Ultimately, Cole's pursuits don't reflect a sense of value creation, risk and reward, or the common good.

Not to say that Cole's not a good dude. I have no idea. I've never met him. And if your daughter got engaged to him five years from now you would probably think she was all set (and your grandkids would be good at math).

Our culture of achievement has grown to emphasize visions of success that are, for the most part, fairly predictable. Cole skipped a couple of steps. The basic plan is to go to Goldman Sachs, McKinsey, or the like, then maybe to a top-ranked business school, then back to banking, consulting, private equity, hedge funds, or a name-brand tech company.

Or maybe go from law school to top firm to partner or in house at an investment firm, and live in New York, San Francisco, Boston, or Washington, DC.*

Again, these institutions and roles are necessary, and they're natural developments in our economy. We need them. But we need people doing other things too. We need people willing to take risks and, yes, to occasionally fail. Like real-world consequences fail. We need people committed over extended periods of time to creating value, no matter how hard that is. We need people who care deeply about the work they're doing.

Imagine someone who you think could stand to take on some risk—someone well educated who would always have something to fall back on, whose family might have some resources so he would be unlikely to starve. And this person would probably be young and free of major life obligations. Someone sort of like . . . Cole.

What's interesting is that many of the people I meet who are young, highly educated, and from good families are among the most risk-averse. They feel like they need to be making progress along a ladder with each passing month or year. Their parents have often set high expectations for them. They measure themselves each period against their peers, who are generally following various well-defined paths.

Yet, as Reid Hoffman, the founder of LinkedIn, and others

---

*There's also the path of going to med school, becoming a surgeon or other specialist and performing procedures three or four days a week. We have an acute shortage of primary care physicians because the achievers we cultivate to be doctors adopt rational incentives: if they specialize they'll make more money and likely work fewer hours than if they're frontline doctors who see patients every day.

have pointed out, remarkable careers are unlikely to advance in a straightforward, linear fashion.[1] They are more likely to contain breakout opportunities that lead to unusually rapid gains (and, of course, relative dips and plateaus).

We need smart and hardworking people to build businesses around the country as much as or more than we need them to do anything else. We need more intelligent risk takers and value creators who see their communities reflected in the work they do. We need to restore the culture of achievement to include value creation, risk and reward, and the common good so that more of our top people are in position to create new enterprises and opportunities.

If we succeed in this, our best and brightest will build the engines of future economic growth. If we don't, our talent will continue to heed purely market-based incentives, our economy will likely continue to underperform, and our culture will become more and more bifurcated.

I just had a son. I'd like him to be very well educated. But I don't want him to necessarily enter a parallel universe where everyone is smart, well paid, and well dressed while the rest of the country wonders where the jobs went.

This is easy to say, but very hard to achieve. People like Cole have every factor turning them toward their current choices; they're heavily recruited and offered money, prestige, training, a network, community, and opened doors. Expecting people like Cole to completely ignore these inducements is unrealistic.

What would the ideal be? There's a renewable energy startup in Providence, Rhode Island, called VCharge that probably could have used Cole too. Its chief science officer,

Jessica Millar, has a PhD in math from MIT. VCharge is trying to make our energy grid more efficient, using energy storage and transmission algorithms. It's not a sure thing, but if it succeeds we'll all be better off for it.

How could you get Cole to head to VCharge instead of to the hedge fund? First, you would hope that immediate income maximization is not the main driver—maybe Cole has a longer time horizon, believes he can make money down the road, and thinks that tinkering with the power grid sounds interesting. Maybe he even has an instinct toward value creation, building things, and having an impact. And second, you could employ resources to recruit him and offer him prestige, training, network, a community, and open doors to head in that direction. You could make it a rational, principled choice as opposed to a vague hope that he decides to do something value creating.

One entrepreneur I met said, "You don't want to be in the army, you want to be an arms dealer." He meant that you want to build a business that doesn't rely upon someone winning or losing but that would benefit from supplying both sides (say, a component manufacturer like Qualcomm that sells to all smartphones, as opposed to a smartphone manufacturer that has to duke it out in competition with the others). The quote sounded smart, but I've concluded that if our young people all follow his advice, we're sunk.

One reason the finance business is always busy is that it functions much like the arms dealer. You don't need to figure out precisely who's going to win or lose. You wait until a business gets to a certain point, and then you help them access capital in the form of equity or debt, give them a credit line, and help them get acquired. And if a company goes down, you're there to assist with reorganizations, divestitures, and bankruptcies.

Yet the real innovation and value are being created by the fighters who are forming little squads and cobbling together businesses. Some fail, some succeed. If they succeed, they wind up building an army that's providing new software, better services, tastier food, or whatever else the world needs. They also create organizations that form the character of the people in the army who believe in what they're doing.

Which would you rather have, better arms dealers or better fighters? And which should our young people want to be? Personally, I always dreamed about going into the woods and fighting the dragon, not selling the guy a sword.

10

Building a Machine to Fix the Machine

It was 2011, and I was the president of Manhattan Prep. I had an employment agreement with our new parent company. I was being paid and treated well. But I had a growing urge to try and solve a problem that, through my work, had become clearer and clearer to me over the years. An army of brilliant ambitious young people was being systematically underutilized and even misallocated. I was certain they could do a lot more for our economy if they were given the opportunity.

In 2008, I had visited Brown for an alumni panel on entrepreneurship and met Charlie Kroll. On the panel, Charlie related how he started his company as a senior in college after not being hired by Morgan Stanley. After years of struggling, his company had grown to have millions of dollars in revenue and employed one hundred people in Providence and beyond. I said to Charlie, "That's incredible. If you had gotten that offer, those one hundred jobs wouldn't exist!" Charlie and I became friends; among other things we have in common, we share the same birthday. And his story stuck in my mind as the answer to questions that had been percolating in my mind for years around what was possible if our smart people were asked to build things.

Over the years, dozens of Teach for America alumni auditioned to teach for Manhattan GMAT. Their lives fascinated me. Brett Beach-Kimball, a brilliant young Wesleyan grad from the suburbs of Washington, DC, had worked with Teach for America in south Texas, married a local, and then moved to San Antonio to become the head of a nonprofit. Miki Litmanovitz, literally a rocket scientist, had graduated from Caltech as an aerospace engineer and worked for Teach for America in San Jose, California, before shifting toward education policy. It was amazing how Teach for America had set such talented people on different courses, in many cases changing their lives and careers. And it was clear that there was a surplus demand; almost ten times as many people applied to Teach for America as actually became corps members. In 2012, Teach for America received almost 50,000 applications for 5,800 spots—it was the number-one employer at Yale, Duke, Columbia, and many other top schools.

I knew firsthand how difficult it is to start a business in your twenties with little in the way of experience or resources. But it was obvious that the most pressing issue facing our country was a return to economic vitality and job growth. For all the talk about entrepreneurship, the statistics showed that the lion's share of top graduates were still heading down the same well-worn paths. As the head of a test-prep company, I'd seen it each day and knew it all too well.

I thought about how to address what I saw as this basic, pressing concern—that the bulk of our best and brightest were not solving the problems of our time. We needed new jobs and innovation, yet we weren't channeling our talent in those directions. It occurred to me that we needed a Teach for America program for entrepreneurship.

I felt very lucky to have had my career work out all right after all of the ups and downs. I wanted to see if I could help make this path easier for others. My parents came to the United States from Taiwan to make a better life. I wanted to do something to give back to the country that had given my family so much. I mean, here I was, a moderately rich dude in my mid-thirties and I hadn't had to kill anyone or sell any organs or anything. The United States is still great, and we need to keep it that way. I felt that if I dedicated a number of years I could help make it so that my kids would grow up in a prosperous country where opportunities are yet expanding.

I began talking to people about this idea, which I called Venture for America—the most self-explanatory name I could think of. It would be a nonprofit with a three-part mission:

To revitalize American cities and communities through entrepreneurship.

To enable our best and brightest to create new opportunities for themselves and others.

To restore the culture of achievement to include value creation, risk and reward, and the common good.

Initially I'd tried to imagine how to solve the problem as a business—perhaps one could set up a for-profit talent recruitment agency or boot camp. But it didn't quite add up; most startups would resist headhunting fees, which can be as high as 20 percent of a starting salary. And asking recent college grads to pay or shoulder further debt seemed equally unrealistic and unappealing. I thought it would be better to raise money as a nonprofit from people and institutions that believed this was a problem worth solving.[*]

Our immediate goal would be to help create 100,000 new US jobs by 2025. To do that, we would provide to startups and growth companies around the country the talent they needed to expand and hire; and we would train a critical mass of our best and brightest to become business builders and entrepreneurs. We would recruit top college graduates who were aspiring entrepreneurs and send them to work at startups around the country for two years, both to contribute and to develop. Venture Fellows would attend a five-week training camp so they'd become friends and colleagues. They'd move in groups to each city and live near each other. The companies would agree to pay these Fellows a base salary of around $35,000 to $38,000, subject to increases. At the end of the two years, Venture for America would invest $100,000 or more in seed funding in Fellows who wanted to start businesses. We would also build an Investment Council of investors who would agree to meet with the Fellows to vet and invest in their business ideas. Over time, past Fellows would start businesses and hire others out of the program. We would give rise to a virtuous cycle of innovation, business building, and job creation.

This was the plan. Everyone who heard about it loved it. The most common reaction was, "What a great idea—why doesn't

---

[*] Going the nonprofit route meant I wasn't going to make much money for a while. I said to Evelyn, "Hey, baby, how about I spend the next five-plus years building a nonprofit?" Thankfully, she's a very good sport.

that exist already?" My friends who worked in investment banking said, "Wow, I would have one hundred percent done a program like that out of college." We were going to build the path we all wished had existed when we were younger.

Still, as we know, enthusiasm is one thing, making it happen is another. I started having "summits" at Manhattan Prep, where I'd invite entrepreneur or investor friends and contacts to the office on a Wednesday night. I set up a boardroom, with bottles of water and notebooks to look classy, and presented a PowerPoint deck on why the need was so strong for Venture for America. At the end of each presentation I asked if each attendee would like to become involved with this amazing new organization, which was going to help create 100,000 new US jobs by 2025.

By the spring of 2011 I'd managed to assemble a pretty impressive list of potential board members and supporters. Some were old friends of mine. Robin Chan and I had met playing basketball at the gym at Columbia. Robin had gone on to become a successful entrepreneur and angel investor, selling his company to Zynga in 2010 and investing in Twitter, Square, and Foursquare. LeRoy Kim, a managing director at Allen and Company, was another friend who cared about the direction of the country. Each enthusiastically took up the cause.

Some were people I knew through Manhattan GMAT. Jeremy Shinewald ran mbaMission, a consulting company that we'd partnered with for years. Jeremy joined up and introduced Venture for America (VFA) to his friends Darren MacDonald, CEO of Pronto Networks, and Eric Cantor, a successful entrepreneur and investor who had founded and sold two Internet infrastructure companies. I'd become friendly with John Delbridge, the cofounder and CEO of Mimeo, a leading online printing company, because my company spent tens of thousands of dollars on printing through Mimeo each month. John and I spoke about how he was always looking for smart people for his company, which had offices in Newark, New Jersey, and Memphis, Tennessee. John joined VFA over lunch. Michael Kahan ran Northpeak Capital, a small private equity firm that had been interested in acquiring Manhattan Prep. I had lunch with Michael and said, "I think I know what's gone wrong with the economy and how to fix it." Michael joined days later and brought in an old colleague of his, Dan Rosenthal, a hedge fund executive who had worked as a venture capitalist and entrepreneur.

Some supporters were friends of friends. I was introduced to Dan Porter, the former president of Teach for America and CEO of OMGPOP, through a mutual friend.* At first Dan was skeptical, in part because he got approached by people who wanted to build the next Teach for America all the time. But he showed up to a summit and, after getting a sense of the organization, agreed to help. Another friend later introduced me to Cameron Breitner of CVC Capital, who became the first chairman of VFA.

Finally, some people wanted to be involved just upon hearing about what we were building. Andy Weissman of Union Square Ventures read about VFA and made a personal donation; his favorite thing is to help budding entrepreneurs develop and succeed. Mat Farkash of Blueprint Health made

---

*OMGPOP, the creator of Draw Something, the successful social media drawing game, was acquired by Zynga for approximately $180 million in 2012.

it his mission to get me in front of every influential friend he had. It felt like the universe had started lending me a hand.

The first Venture for America board members was an exciting group of very smart, capable, well-resourced individuals. It was also, unfortunately, a guyfest, something I hoped to address over time.[1]

There were a few things I learned through the process of assembling the VFA board:

1. Talk to everyone you know. Some people will surprise you. In many cases, friends made an introduction that led to someone joining the board or supporting VFA in a significant way. Say yes to any offer of help or introduction. If you make enough overtures, you'll likely experience some serendipity.

2. Relationships grow and get stronger. People think that you get stuff because you know people. But it's just as true that you develop relationships because you ask for help. Asking is a means of initiating or strengthening a relationship. Some people get anxious about asking for things, but builders see it for what it is—an invitation.

3. Focus on genuine enthusiasm. Some people will be superexcited about the organization. You'd rather have someone involved who is passionate and will go to bat for you than someone who might have a very big name but will be busy or unresponsive.

4. The buy-in is just the beginning. Even after others sign up to help your organization, their role will wax and wane depending upon what you need and their other responsibilities. You need to communicate enough to be transparent and keep them energized (without going overboard). Think of everyone as being on a spectrum and know that relationships are built over the long haul.

5. Expect some adversity. It's a whole lot easier to get people to a meeting than it is to get a meaningful commitment. You should expect any number of disappointing encounters that go nowhere for every one that becomes significant (it's a little bit like dating). Even those who agree to something may later become preoccupied elsewhere. Don't take negative responses or inaction to heart; if you keep making progress people can always jump on board later.

After conducting summits and meetings for a few months, I raised commitments for $350,000, including $120,000 that I put in to seed the organization. I also agreed to forgo salary for a year to stretch resources and help with fund-raising. It seemed like enough to get started.

I began looking for teammates. One of Evelyn's friends from college, Eileen Lee, had left her job as a senior consultant at Accenture. She'd become a consultant directly out of school and was looking for a very different experience. She agreed to come aboard as chief operating officer, which in those early days meant she was working from home and helping organize resources. Later Mike Tarullo, a Duke University alumnus who had been a manager at a staffing startup in New York, joined us. Mike was already a talent expert, having connected and placed hundreds of young professionals with startups around the country. Eddie Shiomi, the former director of training at another fellowship program, Coro, soon joined, as did Megan Hurlburt, who had just graduated as valedictorian at the College of Charleston. It was an excellent early team.

I thought about cities where we could launch and began reaching out to friends for appropriate introductions. Providence seemed like a perfect place to start. Charlie Kroll, my inspiration and birthday brother, agreed to lead the charge. I spent some time with Charlie in Providence getting a sense of the company environment, meeting with exciting companies like Swipely (small business analytics), ShapeUp (employee wellness software), and others. It's a lot of fun meeting with startup founders and leaders who are building innovative organizations—they're extraordinarily easy to root for. Thanks to Charlie, Brown agreed to host our first training camp in 2012, and the Rhode Island Foundation became our first foundation donor.

Next up was Detroit. A friend of Charlie's, Liz Hamburg, introduced me to Bernie Sucher, a Detroit native who was living in Moscow as a financier and entrepreneur. Bernie has had a storied career—he'd worked on Wall Street, started a series of successful businesses in Russia, helped rebuild a local hospital there, was named an Aspen Crown Fellow, and later led Merrill Lynch and Bank of America's offices in Moscow. We met for the first time at the Detroit airport; Bernie agreed to chauffeur and accompany me to meetings as I pitched local startups on Venture for America. Bernie is six foot five, with a shaved head, and was wearing a suit and overcoat when we met. To complicate matters, his only business card was in Russian. We made quite the pair going into offices; he looked like my bodyguard. At least one entrepreneur confided in me later that after we left he'd immediately said, "Who the hell were those guys?" and Googled Bernie to make sure his own life hadn't been in danger. We met with companies like Benzinga (online financial media),

Are You a Human (Captcha replacement), Accio Energy (next-generation wind power generators), and others. After hearing me talk about Venture for America all day, Bernie agreed to join as a board member and has been an enormous champion of VFA ever since.

I wouldn't realize it until months later, but Dan Gilbert funded many of the enterprises we visited on that trip, in part or entirely. Dan is the billionaire entrepreneur founder and chairman of Quicken Loans, the owner of the Cleveland Cavaliers, and a proud Detroit native. He has invested heavily in Detroit, moving 7,500 Quicken Loans employees into downtown office buildings, buying real estate, and giving employees a $20,000 gift for home purchases if they live in Detroit for five years. Dan is doing all he can to bring back his home city, including financing dozens of new businesses and starting a nonprofit, Bizdom U, that helps fledgling entrepreneurs in both Detroit and Cleveland get their start. Dan also cofounded Detroit Venture Partners to invest in local tech companies. Josh Linkner and Jake Cohen from Detroit Venture Partners were among the people Bernie and I met with who became early supporters and partners.

It was the first time I'd been in Detroit; previously I'd just seen magazine montages and the like. I found it fascinating and invigorating. In some Detroit neighborhoods there's a visible line between new businesses on the one hand and abandonment on the other. The entrepreneurs, developers, businesses, and residents in Detroit are literally engaged in a block-by-block, building-to-building fight to rebuild the city's economy and reclaim vacant structures. Everyone there is pulling for everyone else to succeed.

Bernie told me how he'd bought a 1,500-square-foot apartment in Detroit in a high-end co-op building for $20,000.* That's not a misprint—he paid fourteen dollars per square foot to *own*, not rent. The same apartment in Manhattan would have cost sixty to eighty times as much. Jon Zemke, an enterprising University of Michigan grad, was buying houses for $30,000 or so, rehabbing them himself, and renting them out. He's now up to twenty units after starting with only his credit cards. I met Torya Blanchard, who had opened a creperie in downtown Detroit after teaching French in a local public school for five years. Torya cashed out her 401k for $20,000 in 2008 to open her first location, only forty-eight square feet, in the depths of the recession. Today her business is thriving, having expanded to two thousand square feet, and she recently opened a French small-plate bistro and bar called Rodin across the street. Torya's story shows that you don't need much to get started. Detroit was like the new American frontier, with unsettled and abundant cheap land.

Someone told me, "If you like Detroit, you should definitely check out New Orleans." I went down to New Orleans and met with the entrepreneurs there to see if they'd be receptive to a squad of top college grads who wanted to learn how to build a company. Chris Schultz of Launchpad and Voodoo Ventures welcomed me with open arms, introducing me to Matt Wisdom, CEO of Turbosquid (and a fellow Brown alumnus, it turned out) and Tim Williamson, founder of Idea Village.† Turbosquid is like Getty Images for 3-D models—if you need

---

*The maintenance cost was $1,000 per month. The building has a pool and a doorman, and is quite imposing.

†A fun fact: Leonardo DiCaprio's house in the film *Django Unchained* is, in real life, Matt's house. Quentin Tarantino showed up at Matt's doorstep and said, "We need to shoot my next movie here!" Matt happily obliged.

a 3-D image for a website, game, or video, you license it from Turbosquid—while Idea Village is a nonprofit organization that supports entrepreneurship in New Orleans. Chris also introduced me to Patrick Comer, the CEO of Federated Sample, which aggregates online population samples, thus allowing companies to more efficiently run marketing focus groups.

My time in Providence, Detroit, and New Orleans made it clear that there were startup companies in each with a need and desire for young, hungry talent to grow their companies. Each city had a budding startup scene, fueled by Betaspring (a Providence-based startup accelerator), Detroit Venture Partners, and Idea Village. More important, I found that the men and women who started and ran companies in these cities were often high-character, high-integrity people. They were genuine builders. They typically had their heads down and were working out of the spotlight, and had a natural interest in developing the next generation of entrepreneurs in their own backyard. I couldn't wait to get them some talented aspiring entrepreneurs in training to take under their wings.

I left Manhattan Prep in May 2011. Dan Gonzalez succeeded me as president, so I knew the company was in good hands. We had a Venture for America press launch and a party, both of which were picked up by Techcrunch, Fast Company, *Barron's*, the *Huffington Post*, Fox News, and other media outlets. We wanted to get the word out to potential recruits that there was a new path for aspiring entrepreneurs. Recruiting the right young people was going to be the most important driver of our success.

I went on a college tour from September through November 2011 and visited thirty-two different college campuses to conduct information sessions, from Brown and Cornell to UVA and Duke to UT Austin and Vanderbilt to UC Berkeley and Stanford to Vassar and MIT to the University of Michigan and Tulane and on and on. I saw many parts of the country I had never visited before. Often, the university grounds were a step up from the surrounding areas, and you could feel the difference as soon as you set foot on campus. I would go into each information session armed with a PowerPoint deck. At each stop, I asked the students, "What do you want in a first job?"

Common answers were, "To develop skills," "To keep my options open," "To do interesting work," "To work with other smart people," "To gain some real responsibility," "For money," and "To do something good for society."

I asked them to tell me the six default paths for people who graduated from their college; they could pretty easily name finance, management consulting, law school, med school, grad school, and Teach for America. They could also identify the primary destinations for most students: New York, San Francisco, Boston, and Washington, D.C (with Chicago thrown in if I was in the Midwest).

I then said, "Most of you probably had never heard of management consulting or investment banking before you showed up at school. Why do you think your classmates are doing those things now?" Responses were, "They come and recruit us," "They're safe," "Prestige," "They look good on a résumé," "It's good training, " "Because of their parents," "These jobs open doors," "These jobs keep options open," "Money," "To pay off school loans," "To network," "To make connections," and "Because they want to do something important."

These responses were consistent everywhere I went. I then asked, "How many of you are interested in either starting your own company or joining a startup?" Most hands went up, given that the information session was billed as either Venture for America or as an "entrepreneurship" seminar.

"Okay. And yet most of you aren't actually going to join a startup when you graduate. Why not?" The common answers were, "Because I was not recruited," "It's hard to find a startup," "It's risky," "Startups have no money," and "I don't know where to start."

At this point I'd close the loop. I'd tell them that Venture for America would combine the prestige, training, network, and connections of professional services with the chance to work at a startup and even the possibility of some seed money, and that they should consider applying and also tell their friends about it.[2]

Between two and two hundred people attended each presentation, though the number was generally a whole lot closer to the former. Sometimes it felt as if I'd spend a whole day and night on the road to talk to one student. But at each campus, at least a few attendees said, "Wow, this is exactly what I've been looking for!" Many felt constrained to only a small number of choices coming out of school and were looking for an alternative. I met students who seemed bright and talented and wanted to apply, and that was enough to keep me energized.

We were looking for very specific candidates who could amplify the chances of a startup or growth company succeeding and hiring more employees. As a result, we weren't trying to drive numbers so much as quality. They didn't necessarily need to have started a business or be able to code in various programming languages, though that would be great. Instead, we were looking for "adaptive excellence"—individuals with high records of achievement in some combination of academic, athletic, extracurricular, personal, and business contexts. If you are the captain of the national champion rugby team, someone with a 4.0 grade point average in engineering physics, the president of the student body, the first in your family to go to college, someone who has run a business and supervised twenty people, these are all good signs that you'll be above average at addressing the litany of challenges facing you at a startup. VFA believed that talent, work ethic, attitude, and character were transferable to the early-stage business setting like any other, and sought motivated people who demonstrated the ability to be successful in whatever they'd done to date.

I was quick to discourage people who didn't seem very serious. The last thing I wanted was for people to somehow back into VFA; they had to want it 100 percent.

During one of my brief periods back in New York, a friend contacted me and said he had a pass to an *Economist* conference he couldn't use. I went and wound up meeting two people who would change the course of Venture for America—Tony Hsieh, CEO of Zappos, and Jeff Weiner, CEO of LinkedIn.

In startup circles, Tony Hsieh is a bit of a legend. He sold his first company to Microsoft for over $250 million in his twenties, then became the lead investor in and CEO of Zappos.com, which was acquired by Amazon for over $1 billion. His book *Delivering Happiness*, which describes how culture can be a company's competitive advantage, became a best seller. And Zappos.com makes thousands of people happy every day.

Tony invested $350 million of his own money in an initiative, Downtown Project, to turn downtown Las Vegas into a thriving community: $200 million in real estate, $50 million in tech startups, $50 million in local small businesses, and $50 million in arts, education, and culture. He's also moving over a thousand Zappos employees from the suburbs into the old downtown city hall, which he's renovating (after buying it from the city for $18 million). One staffer described the transition as being "from Sin City to Sim City." It's one of the most incredible initiatives in the country, and it's basically what you wish every centimillionaire would do—decide to positively impact an entire city.

I introduced myself and said to Tony, "We love what you're doing! We can help bring a squad of smart killers to work with you in Vegas." He was interested enough to give me his contact information, and we met in Vegas months later. In the spring of 2012, his team hired seven Venture Fellows for Downtown Project. Tony would later speak at our first summer celebration and go on CNBC to announce a pledge of $1 million to support Venture for America, our first commitment at that level.

Jeff Weiner had tweeted a Techcrunch article about Venture for America a couple of weeks before I met him. Under Jeff's leadership, LinkedIn has become one of the most highly regarded companies of this era; its online network has expanded to include over 200 million professionals. Months after our first conversation, I met with Jeff at his offices in Mountain View, California. He told me that he liked what we were doing because he'd had a similar idea for an organization he was going to call Venturecorps years earlier. I said,

"Jeff, you can live vicariously through us!" He became an adviser to VFA and funded and mentored four Venture Fellows as they started a nonprofit, the Startup Effect, to train eighth-graders in entrepreneurship in Detroit and New Orleans.

During this first year the *New York Times*, *Time* magazine, the *Wall Street Journal*, and *USA Today* each wrote a story about Venture for America. The press and networking were an adjustment for me—I'd been operating in relative anonymity for the past ten years (something that can be said for 99 percent of businesses). From my Stargiving days I was doubtful about the value of press, and Manhattan GMAT had grown robustly for years without much press attention, so my skepticism had deepened.

I quickly realized that for a nonprofit it was different; press and goodwill matter a lot. Everyone involved—from staff to applicants to donors to sponsors—enjoys the sense that others care about what the organization is doing. You ask people for things all of the time, and they need to be motivated by the sense that the organization is up to something big.

Goodwill is much more likely to happen in person. When we were starting out, I was looking for ways to avoid what I regarded as the event trap—nonprofits would spend $200,000 on an event to raise $300,000. I thought to myself, "That's silly. Why not just get the $300,000 and skip the event?" Then, when I tried it, I realized that people would much rather give money if they can show up to something and experience what the organization is doing. You've got to go to people or gather them together.

The biggest adjustment for me was that VFA, like most

nonprofits, had to speak to at least two audiences and the feedback mechanism wasn't direct. In the nonprofit world, there's service delivery (in our case, recruiting top college graduates, training and mentoring them, and placing them at startups and growth companies) and then there's fund-raising. They're two very different activities with different competencies and audiences. It reminded me a bit of balancing investors and customers, but on a much more dramatic scale.

I was used to feedback that was direct, immediate, and appropriately self-reinforcing—most businesses are like this. Let's say you have a business selling chocolate chip cookies. People tell you, "Mmm-mmm! Your cookies are delicious!" They show you how much they like the cookies by buying them, telling their friends, and so on. Your business grows, and you spend the money on more cookie stands, better marketing, and different and improved recipes, among other things.

In the nonprofit world the feedback is much more indirect. To stretch the example above, you're giving the cookies away. You then go to donors and say, "Look at these cookies! See how much everyone likes them? You can tell by their expression when they eat them. You should give me the money to bake some more." How many contributions you get is related to the quality of the cookies, but it's also related to what people think of the cookies (without eating them), how good you are at describing the cookies, and how many people you can tell about them. In practice, I found myself saying yes to things that could potentially result in raising VFA's profile and fund-raising opportunities. Raising money was going to be a big part of my job, and the most direct feedback mechanism, but it couldn't be my entire job if VFA was going to succeed. It was easy to see how nonprofits could become overly engrossed with courting and pleasing donors.

Another adjustment in running a nonprofit was that it was harder to reward people financially. The team was excited, and dedicated to achieving our mission. But I found that there was a tendency to rely too heavily on this intrinsic motivation. I felt that we couldn't pay people competitively because we were a nonprofit. At Manhattan GMAT, I had done my best to create a positive work environment and culture, but I also believed in rewarding people financially at or above the market rate for a job well done. At a nonprofit I saw how tempting it would be to rely upon the staff being young, idealistic, and mission-driven. I wanted ambitious, high-efficiency superstars like Eileen, Mike, and Megan to view Venture for America as a place to build their careers for the long haul, which would have to include, in my mind, competitive pay raises.* I didn't believe you could build an organization in which people felt like they had to make serious lifestyle sacrifices or suffer in order to do good work, and still expect it to develop a sustained winning culture. I started thinking about how to make this happen over time.

As buzz grew, organizations from various US cities started reaching out, asking us to expand to their regions. We eventually said yes to Cincinnati, which joined Providence, Detroit, New Orleans, and Las Vegas. Cincinnati's leadership was investing heavily in innovation, with institutions like Cincy-

---

*There's a great TED talk by Dan Pallotta, founder of AIDS Ride, on this subject about how nonprofits function (and ought to). Best eighteen minutes ever if you're interested in charitable orgs. You can see it at www.danpallotta.com.

Tech, the Brandery, and Cintrifuse each dedicating millions of dollars to building an ecosystem of successful startups, with regional foundations and corporate leaders providing support.[*]

When I visited Cincinnati I saw a company called General Nano that manufactures a carbon nanotube material that can be used to make planes more resistant to lightning strikes. The US Navy invested in General Nano through its Office of Naval Research. The military visits Cincinnati regularly, in part because G.E. Aviation, which manufactures airplane components, is based there.

General Nano was different from the businesses I was used to seeing. I realized it was a company that would be unlikely to be founded in, say, New York City. The latest wave of New York startups (e.g., Rent the Runway, Warby Parker, Foursquare, the Gilt Groupe, and others) tends to capitalize on New York's existing industries (fashion, retail, and the like). There are no airplane factories in New York, so there wouldn't be a General Nano there either. Cities tend to produce startups that are either solving local institutions' problems or building on existing strengths.

I began to see the same phenomenon in other cities as well. New Orleans is a haven for education reform as the only city in the United States where more than half of all public school children attend charter schools.[†] Also in New Orleans

---

[*]Eric Avner of the Haile Foundation helped bring us to Cincinnati and was joined by the Greater Cincinnati Foundation in supporting VFA.

[†]In New Orleans, most public schools were converted to charter schools after Hurricane Katrina in 2005, and Teach for America alumni are a big part of the education establishment there.

are 4.0 Schools, a design lab for education innovation, and Kickboard, an analytics and student tracking software company for teachers. Baltimore, the home of Johns Hopkins University, has a cluster of innovative health tech companies such as Reify Health, which uses mobile technology to improve and measure medical treatments; the company was started by four Johns Hopkins medical and graduate students who left school. Baltimore also has cybersecurity start-ups, like Zero FOX that benefit from the city's proximity to Fort Meade and the US Army Cyber Command. Detroit's enterprises build on the region's high concentration of engineers and the presence of the US automakers as well as Quicken Loans.

Aside from building on the strengths of each region, companies in these cities could take advantage of lower costs relative to New York or San Francisco. Investment or savings go farther because office rent is cheaper, salaries are lower, and vendors are less expensive. For a small company, paying $800 per month for an office of 1,200 square feet versus $4,000 a month for the same amount of space in Manhattan makes a difference pretty quickly. Engineers are less expensive (and potentially will stick around longer).* Burn rates

---

* "We felt we couldn't build a long-term company [in Silicon Valley] because of the turnover—not only to get people in the door but retain them," comments Jay Gierak, cofounder of Stik, a social recommendation startup that relocated to Detroit from San Francisco. "It's hard to compete with Facebook and Airbnb but also . . . where there are people whispering in your ear to start a two-person app company. . . . We thought there was a culture in Detroit where we could build a long-term company that was going to win." Stik cofounder Nathan Labenz adds, "We have time to get to know potential hires here. . . . We can take a couple of meetings, work through a code problem together. By the time you do that in Silicon Val-

are lower across the board, providing a longer runway and a greater margin for both error and experimentation.

I was also struck by how far people's incomes went. For $1,000 a month, you could rent a very spacious apartment or a small house for multiple people in many cities. For the same money in New York you would be lucky to live with a roommate in a converted six-hundred-square-foot one-bedroom apartment in an outer borough with a significant commute. I'd found out how difficult it can be, in a higher-cost environment, to maintain a reasonable lifestyle (and your spirits) on a shoestring, particularly as those around you are living large. I imagined how not having to worry as much about day-to-day expenses could help keep your energy up and give you license to take more risks as well as more time to build.

I also saw how those who started a business in a smaller market were likely to get attention and support. They were heavily covered in the local media (newspaper, blogs). Public officials took an interest in what their companies were doing and tried to be supportive in concrete ways, including securing economic development grants and introductions to contacts. Leaders of small companies were asked to speak at local universities, sit on industry panels, participate in local business associations, and so on. They knew everyone else who was building a company and, perhaps more important, everyone who knew them wanted to see them succeed.

As I traveled, I saw a number of enormously successful startups based in nontraditional cities: Zappos.com in Las Vegas, Under Armour in Baltimore, Receivables Exchange

---

ley, the person has already taken a job." See Matt Burns, "From the Valley to the Motor City: Why Stik Moved Back to Detroit," retrieved from http://techcrunch.com/2012/12/10/detroit-two-point-oh/.

in New Orleans, and Audible.com in Newark, New Jersey, demonstrating that innovation and value creation can happen anywhere. It's clearly possible for world-class industry-leading companies to come of age and remain headquartered in places that might have been considered unlikely before the fact—consider Walmart in Bentonville, Arkansas; Procter and Gamble in Cincinnati; Nike in Beaverton, Oregon; FedEx in Memphis, Tennessee; and on and on.

This is not to say that all is ideal in smaller or less-developed startup systems. Angel funding and venture capitalists still congregate in regions that have had numerous exits and positive outcomes (e.g., Silicon Valley, New York, Boston). It can be hard for a startup to get the attention of investors who like to stay in their own backyards. Top-notch engineers, executive talent, programmers, web designers, salespeople, marketing staff, and the like are all difficult to find no matter where you are. It can be that much harder for companies in a market where there aren't as many people with the necessary skills and experience. On the flip side, if a company does find the right person, there probably isn't as much local competition for her. Good companies in these cities were adjusting and building on their advantages while doing their utmost to overcome the gaps.

There's a misconception out there that Silicon Valley is the only place for technology companies to thrive. We all remember Facebook moving out west. But even Mark Zuckerberg said in 2011, "If I were starting now, I would have stayed in Boston," adding, "You don't have to move out here to do this."[3] Silicon Valley is unlikely to produce the same set of companies as New York, Detroit, or Las Vegas because the region has a different set of strengths and defining institutions.

The problems that startups tackle are dramatically different in different regions. After spending time in a range of cities, it was clear to me how much we need geographic diversity in startups in order to drive innovation in aviation, consumer products, education, health, cybersecurity, biotechnology, manufacturing, the automotive industry, and every other economic sector. If only a few US cities attract the talent to become innovation hubs, we'd miss out on most of the opportunities for value creation throughout the country.

I was learning a lot by visiting campuses and startups. Then in April 2012, I got an e-mail with the subject line, "INVITATION: Meeting with the President (4/26)." I opened the e-mail, wondering who they were talking about, when I realized it was from the White House: "We are inviting a small group of our past Champions to participate in a small meeting with the President." I'd been named a Champion of Change by the White House the previous year for starting Venture for America, but this message was completely out of the blue.

After confirming that the e-mail was real, I immediately responded, "Yes, I am able to attend" and forwarded the invite to my family as well as to the VFA board members.

A little over a week later, I was in the White House map room waiting to meet President Obama. It was like being on a movie set, except it was real, complete with Secret Service agents scanning the room for threats. For some reason I had neglected to wear a tie, probably because I'd been spending my time visiting colleges and startups. One of the White House staffers, Ronnie Cho, literally gave me the tie off his neck to save me from being the schmuck who showed up to meet the president without a tie.

The room was abuzz with anticipation. Everyone had one eye on the person she was talking to and one eye on the doorway. When the president arrived, it was as if a dam broke. He said "Hello!" in a friendly voice as he entered the room and began greeting people. As I shook his hand, I thought to myself that his hands were bigger than you'd think, and that it must help him playing basketball.

We talked for about ten minutes. I explained to him what we were doing with Venture for America and he told me how great an idea he thought it was. He asked if I'd spoken yet to Steve Case, the founder of AOL and the head of the Startup America Partnership. He also asked some other questions about the program and the experience over the two years for the Venture Fellows. I'll admit that I found myself playing a role during the meeting, that of "gracious guy visiting the president." It occurred to me that President Obama must play "friendly president" all the time. And then he moved on to the next guest. On my way out, a couple of White House officials gave me their business cards and contact information.

On the train ride back from Washington that night, I thought to myself, "Man, I just met the president! That was a trip. At least now he knows what Venture for America is."

11

The Future Changes for at Least a Few

Entrepreneurship is one of the most common answers to the question of what to do about unemployment in this country. But starting a business, while potentially fulfilling and rewarding, is really hard. You need to be a manager, salesperson, fund-raiser, product designer, tech support expert, customer service representative, and cleaning person all in one. If you're the sort of person who could start a successful business, you could generally pretty easily get a job. It's a *lot* easier to get a job than to start a business. Expecting unemployed people to whip up jobs for themselves, even if one were to supply support, training, and infrastructure, is an unrealistic proposition most of the time. People who have no safety nets and limited access to resources may not be equipped to take on the additional risks and responsibilities necessary to start a new organization.

Everything surrounding entrepreneurship is easier than the thing itself. Supporting it, talking about it, investing in it, accelerating or incubating it, teaching it, studying it, and holding a conference about it are a whole lot easier than actually building a new business.* Large corporations spend millions on innovation initiatives and research and development and come up empty for a reason; the new development process is intrinsically inefficient and unpredictable.

Even if you have everything in place in terms of a founding team, capital, and opportunity, there's no guarantee that a business is going to work. But it helps a lot if you can stick with it and have some things going for you. If anything, we need our most eminently employable people to start and run companies—people who are at the top of the pyramid in terms of skills, exposure, credibility, resources, talents, character, persistence, know-how, networks, cultural capital, and the like. They can struggle a bit, scrape their knees, learn, get better, and come back stronger. It's this sort of person who can more easily gather resources to build an organization that can in turn hire other people.

It was the fall of 2011, and Mike Mayer had a choice to make. He had just received an offer from the investment banking division of Credit Suisse in New York. At the age of twenty-two, he'd be an analyst with a base salary of $70,000 and a chance for a bonus of the same amount. It was supposed to be the culmination of his entire college career.

Mike had grown up in the suburbs of Orlando, Florida, the son of a doctor and a behavior therapist. He was the valedictorian of his high school and played three sports—baseball, basketball, and golf. He was the sort of person who naturally looked to make those around him happy, and that had

---

*I'd include this book in this list—it's also easier to write about it than to do it.

helped get him named "most likely to succeed" in his high school class. He went to the Wharton School of Business at the University of Pennsylvania and decided to study finance because that's what everyone else did, and it seemed highly practical. He excelled, getting a 3.9 grade point average in one of the most competitive programs in the country.

In the fall of his junior year at Wharton, Mike saw the majority of his classmates begin to interview for finance internships and management consulting jobs. He was at one of the most intensely recruited college campuses, and the pressure was high. Mike practiced for his interviews and networked as hard as anyone. In the hierarchy of opportunities, the internship he landed at Credit Suisse was considered to be among the best.

He'd enjoyed his summer in New York at Credit Suisse—many of his friends were around, and together they explored the Big Apple after hours. Mike felt he'd gotten something out of some aspects of the work; he felt he understood the inner workings of the finance world much more comprehensively now, and he'd acquired new skills in PowerPoint and Excel.

However, his investment banking analyst position at Credit Suisse didn't feel quite like what he'd been looking for. He thought it would be meaningful, but producing models and pitch decks for potential deals and clients left him feeling kind of removed from the real world. For most of his life, Mike had thought that he might want to start his own business one day, and everyone told him that finance was great training for that. Yet what he'd seen of investment banking made him skeptical that his lifelong pursuit would ever materialize if he stayed in banking.

Still, it was a great job offer. His parents were supportive and told him to do what he felt was best. His friends pretty much said, "Dude, take it. That's a sweet deal." Plus, there was the big question: If he decided not to take the job offer, what else was he going to do?

Around the same time, Kathy Cheng was weighing an offer from an economic consulting firm in New York City. Kathy had studied economics and urban planning at MIT, and it seemed like a good job—one directly aligned with her studies.

Kathy had grown up in nearby New Jersey. Both of her parents had studied computer science and were working in the field. She'd done well in school and studied hard, had always been near the top of her class. Yet she also harbored a bit of a creative streak. She picked up whatever instruments she had access to and wrote songs in order to channel her need to create something.

Kathy had spent the summer before her senior year interning at the US Small Business Administration in Washington, DC, researching ways to help small companies succeed. While she was there, her boss, Ellen Kim, mentioned a brand-new program called Venture for America. The program was launching in Detroit, New Orleans, and Providence, and its short-term goal was to help create 100,000 new US jobs by 2025.

Kathy was intrigued. She wasn't sure how her parents would react to the idea of setting aside a perfectly reasonable job offer and moving to a city like Detroit. But she felt that the best way to learn about business was to actually be inside of one as opposed to writing reports about them. She submitted her application to Venture for America without talking to her parents about it. A couple of months later, after a multi-stage series of submissions, video and in-person interviews, and participation in selection day, she got a call. She was in.

Andy Chatham loved business. He discovered this during his sophomore year at Cornell University when he took a job managing a shipping and storage company. He spent a year running a business that operated in the physical world with people, boxes, trucks, and warehouses.

A couple years later, he found himself running Cornell Student Agencies—the oldest student-run business in the country. He was responsible for operating seven student-run businesses and over $10 million in mixed-use real estate. Budgeting and bringing in over $3 million in revenue over the course of the school year had a profound impact on his worldview.

He obsessed over providing a positive experience each day to twenty direct reports and thousands of customers. When something went wrong (which it often did in businesses run by nineteen-year-olds) Andy was responsible for fixing it and reporting to a board of directors. He hired, fired, and evaluated the performance of his peers and adults years older than himself. He would be the first person to tell you that 90 percent of what he learned in college was outside the classroom.

Andy had grown up in Rhode Island. His father was a marketing executive at a small tech company in Providence and a self-proclaimed geek. He taught Andy the importance of taking pride in one's own work and tried to impart some of his detail-oriented, perfectionist attitude to his son.

It was important to Andy that the first thing he did after

Cornell would be something that got him closer to someday owning his own business—maybe not tomorrow, but not when he was fifty, either. He applied to positions at consulting firms and investment banks because it was what those around him were doing as college seniors.

After many interviews, he received an offer from a large software consulting company to enter their corporate sales training program. He'd be based in a suburb of New York City. It was a good opportunity, and he was sure that he'd get some great skills.

On the other hand, he also had just been offered a fellowship from Venture for America the week before. His father thought that VFA represented a tremendous opportunity. But Andy was wavering—it seemed like a big decision.

He was on his way to class when his cell phone rang. He answered. "Hello, this is Andy."

The voice on the other end was familiar. "Hello, Andy. This is Sheldon Whitehouse." Andy was dumbstruck for a second. Really? Sheldon Whitehouse was one of Rhode Island's senators! Andy had interned for his office a couple of summers earlier, but had never had a real conversation with him. What was Whitehouse doing calling him out of the blue?

Andy recovered quickly. "Hello, Senator."

"I'm here in my office with Andrew Yang. He thinks it's important that you join Venture for America. It seems like a great program."

Andy paused, then responded, "Wow. I see. Yes, it does."

"Wanted to call and let you know. Hope we see you back in Rhode Island."

"Yes, sir. I hope so too."

"Great to hear. Thank you, Andy. Be well."

"Thank you, Senator."

And with that the call ended. "That was pretty crazy," Andy thought. "Dad will get a kick out of that." He accepted the offer from Venture for America a few days later.[*]

The combination of press, word of mouth, and the campus tour worked. By the spring of 2012, hundreds of college seniors and recent graduates had applied to Venture for America in our first year for the chance to help create jobs and revitalize America through entrepreneurship. Applicants underwent a three-round process that included an extensive online submission, phone interview, and video interview. Finalists were invited to a selection day in New York, where they were put in teams and asked to complete a set of assignments in real time in front of a panel of experienced judges.[†]

Reading through submissions and interviewing and meeting hundreds of young people was an education in itself. We encountered something of a gap between what students were studying and a concrete role in an organization.

For example, we often encountered a generalized desire to do something positive framed as "social entrepreneurship," "environmental sustainability," or "international development," with little sense of what that would mean in practice. Some conveyed a feeling they had picked up in school:

---

[*] It was pure coincidence that I happened to be meeting with Senator Whitehouse at the time that Andy was still considering our offer. The senator's a good sport.

[†] For our first big selection day, our initial space fell through and we had to scramble. Thanks to Greg Gushee, a real estate developer friend, we wound up holding it on the fortieth floor of a brand-new Manhattan apartment building that had yet to open. The toilets didn't have seats on them, which confused everyone, but the view was magnificent.

businesses = not so great; social entrepreneurship or triple-bottom-line businesses or nonprofits = good. And this in turn had shaped their goals.

I wished I could somehow deliver the message that it's not about an organization's legal or tax structure; it's about a company's leadership, how it creates value, and how it conducts itself. There are for-profit businesses delivering tremendous value to the world (Google, Amazon, LinkedIn, and that place on the corner that makes incredibly addictive sandwiches), and poorly run nonprofits doing very little.

I now run a nonprofit, so I obviously believe that tax-exempt organizations can serve incredibly useful roles and create value. The issue with nonprofits is that they tend to be small and have difficulty growing. Over 82 percent of all filing nonprofits in the United States had budgets of less than $1 million in 2010, a figure that has remained unchanged for years.[1] From 1970 through 2009, only 144 nonprofits crossed the $50 million annual revenue barrier; in the same period, 46,136 for-profit businesses surpassed that mark.[2] Revenue isn't the perfect measurement for a nonprofit organization's impact, but the contrast gives one a sense of the trajectory of different types of organizations. Nonprofit and philanthropy budgets are tied to the percentage of US gross domestic product (GDP) that is donated each year. This figure has been relatively constant at about 2 percent of GDP since 1970.[3] The pool of resources available from individuals, corporations, foundations, and government entities is thus fairly fixed or growing at the same rate as the economy (recently, 1–3 percent per year). Meanwhile, 50,000 new nonprofits get formed every year.[4] So every year you have a growing number of nonprofits vying for a fairly constant set of resources;

statistically, a nonprofit that just avoids shrinking is actually performing above average.

In my experience, ambitious young smart people are happier and better utilized in growth organizations. If a nonprofit is on a growth path, then it could be a dynamic opportunity. But most nonprofits aren't rapidly expanding. It's dispiriting being in an environment with scarce resources and little opportunity for advancement; I know many young people who went to stable or shrinking nonprofits who became disillusioned or burned out after several years despite an initial attachment to the missions of the organizations.

Another consistent thread we saw among applicants was an archetype I'll call "the planner." An essay would say something like, "First I'm going to do Venture for America. Then I'm going to get my JD and MBA so I understand law and business. After that I'm going to do something international so I understand globalization. And then I will start an international business or go into economic development." In a way, all of the ambition and desire for self-development was admirable. But you got a sense that they didn't really know what they wanted to do and had come up with a string of abstractions and badges to fill the void (while also seeking a credential for each step).

On the opposite end of the spectrum were people who had already been working on businesses and were looking to Venture for America for a helpful framework and mentorship. They had concrete ideas of the business they'd want to start. They had experienced enough of the million microsteps that are required in building something that they understood what they were getting into. They were people who, if they didn't know how to do something, were smart and determined enough to sit down and figure it out on their own. They had demonstrated some grit and action orientation, not just accomplishment. Some were going to hustle their way to a startup with or without Venture for America. We were looking for people who would be commercially valuable from day one—they could sell, acquire customers, engineer and improve a product or process, or create compelling content—to drive a business forward today and maybe even potentially start one tomorrow.

We extended offers to a small fraction of candidates. Perhaps because of the appeal of the mission and the intensity of the scrutiny throughout, virtually everyone to whom we extended an offer accepted. We then introduced successful candidates to partner startup companies that conducted their own interviews based on our recommendations. We wound up with a first class of forty outstanding Fellows, including, in addition to Mike Mayer, Kathy Cheng, and Andy Chatham,

> Brentt Baltimore—an investment banker at Credit Suisse from Los Angeles who turned down an offer from a private equity firm to join Venture for America;
>
> Ethan Carlson—a Yale mechanical engineer from a small town in Minnesota who wanted to work in clean energy;
>
> Gabby Bryant—an economics major from Harvard who wanted to go back to her hometown of Detroit and do her part to help rebuild the city;
>
> Max Nussenbaum—an ultra-creative Wesleyan grad who had written a play and had competed on *Who Wants to Be a Millionaire?*; and

Tim Dingman—an electrical engineer from Brown who ran a design conference and built websites on the side.

They were joined by thirty-two other top grads, many of whom I'd met during my campus tour.[*]

It was quite a group. When I saw the Fellows all together for the first time, their energy, optimism, and talent were palpable. They were walking, laughing proof that our young people would accept short-term sacrifices in order to develop into the individuals and builders we needed them to become. I couldn't wait to see them get to work.

[*]For a full list of the Venture Fellows for 2012, see appendix E or visit http://www.ventureforamerica.org/2012fellows. It's an inspiring group.

12

Teams of Builders

Who was the eighth employee at Google back in 1999?

I don't know either; I tried to Google it and couldn't find it. But I'm pretty confident that the eighth employee joined before the company was cool, built some amazing things, and had an incredible experience—and is now loaded.

Google is perhaps the most important and influential company in the country today. But most people can only name its founders, Larry Page and Sergey Brin, and maybe its former CEO Eric Schmidt. Same thing with Amazon and Jeff Bezos, Apple and Steve Jobs or Tim Cook, or Starbucks and Howard Schultz. We have a very human tendency to associate large organizations with their leaders, particularly if, as in the cases above, the leader is also the founder. It makes the narrative easy. You can show a picture of the person, interview him or her, and ask for lessons learned. This also shapes people's aspirations; hundreds of books and classes on entrepreneurship exist to teach us how we can be a bit more like these visionary leaders. It's as if Howard is actually running around and opening all of those Starbucks branches in our neighborhoods.

But with every growth company story, there's a whole team of capable, talented, motivated people who have worked for years to make it happen and whose lives have been transformed as a result. It's not just the founder—it's the people who have been a part of the organization throughout its progression. If a company happens to go on to become a household name, as in the cases above, you typically have dozens or hundreds of early employees who have their careers defined by it.

The vast majority of companies don't go public and mint dozens of millionaires. And most companies don't go around doling out stock options; private companies tend to be very tight about ownership. But the same collective transformation is true on a lesser scale with any growth company that makes headway. At Manhattan GMAT, Danielle DiCiaccio started straight out of college in 2006 as an entry-level hire and now runs a whole department. It's very different being a director at a $20 million company from working at a $2 million company—imagine seeing and making that happen throughout your twenties. Moreover, you'd know and trust the people you're working with because you've been a part of the team that built the enterprise to that level.

Sounds great, right? You're thinking, Sign me up! The trick is that by the time it's evident that a company is going to take off, it's often too late to be a big part of the team. If I joined Google today as employee number 53,862, no one would care. But back in the day, Google was no sure thing. Larry and Sergey even offered to sell Google to Excite in

1999 for $1 million, which Excite's CEO turned down at the time (to his eternal regret).

So it's a bit of a bet. You want to join a team before it's cool and hope that the company takes off. If it does, you could have yourself a very good run. You could even wind up being the difference between the company taking off and languishing on a small scale. Maybe you will attain a position of real responsibility—maybe it even gives you a career. If it doesn't work out, you almost certainly will have developed some skills that will make you a contributor for the next thing.

These people—the builders who work with the founders to help these companies grow and prosper—are, in many ways, more appropriate role models. The plan should not be, for the most part, "start a company." More realistically, the plan should be "join a team." If you're positioned to start your own organization, that's great—but rare. You've got an unusual profile.

If you join a growth organization, you'll likely do different things in different roles throughout your career. It's excellent to learn and build with others. You'll meet people you want to work with. If you have a good run, you can always come back and start something later. For example, Alexis Maybank worked at eBay with Jeff Skoll for years. She launched and ran eBay Canada and helped start eBay Motors. Years later, she went on to cofound Gilt Groupe, a major e-commerce company that makes my wife and many others happy.

And it's not just coders and engineers that these new companies need. Just about any growth company is going to need smart salespeople, account and project managers, business development, marketing, operations, customer service, content creation, communications, analytics, and social media.

If I told you that there's a startup company in New York founded in 2005 that has grown to over $1 billion in revenue with over 1,000 employees, you would probably think it must be a tech or finance company. But it's not. It's yogurt maker Chobani, founded by Hamdi Ulukaya, a Turkish immigrant who bought a defunct yogurt plant in New Berlin, New York, in 2005. Now it's the top-selling yogurt in the country (and quite tasty). I'm sure the eighth employee at Chobani is also having a pretty good run.

Make no mistake—it's not easy to find or pick a good team or early-stage company to join. Even professional investors mess this up all the time and they're looking at dozens of companies for a living. You hope to find an outfit with experienced, high-character, capable leaders. As we've seen, even if everything is in place most companies will not achieve their goals. Have confidence that if the company doesn't work out, you will take lessons from the experience and apply them to your next endeavor, giving it a much greater chance for success. People can grow from adversity as much as they do from prosperity.

When the tech bubble burst in 2001, virtually everyone I knew lost his job as companies flamed out right and left—mine included. Some people did something totally random to pay the bills for a while as the smoke cleared (like teach the GMAT). But most everyone bounced back. My friend Robin worked for a company that went under; then he went corporate for a little while, and then years later he started a company that was acquired by Zynga. My friend Brian, who worked with me at Stargiving, also went corporate briefly and later became an independent film producer who produced a successful documentary on a then obscure college basketball player named Jeremy Lin. Another friend whose business went under, Matt, became the cofounder of a tech company called Videolicious that's funded by Amazon.

We'd all gotten in the habit of building things. Sometimes you're the founder, sometimes you're a team member, and sometimes you're just in the vicinity and scheming. But once you become a builder, it's hard to let go.

13

Training Camp, and Notes from the Field

The first ever five-week Venture for America training camp started at Brown University in June 2012. The VFA team and I moved into apartments and dorm rooms in Providence to prepare. It was kind of surreal for me to be living in my old college town sixteen years after graduating. I even ate in the dining hall a couple of times. (It's about the same as I remembered.)

On opening day, I talked to the Fellows about our mission to revitalize US cities and communities through entrepreneurship and restore the culture of achievement. I told them that they've taken on the hardest challenge one can think of—to help create something new that will last and have a sustained impact. I asked them what people thought their strengths were. There was no shortage of responses. The words "smart," "energetic," and "tech-savvy" were thrown around.

I then asked them what people thought their weaknesses were going to be. Here there was more reticence and silence. I reframed it as, "What do companies fear about your generation?" I'd picked up on some of this from talking to startup founders and managers. Some of the descriptions thrown out were "entitled," "high maintenance," "low attention to detail," "unfocused," "short attention span," "low commitment," "lazy," "low perseverance," "inability to withstand adversity or accept criticism," "low self-awareness and sensitivity," "believe they know best," "arrogant," and "self-absorbed, think others exist for their benefit."

"Look," I said. "You should know that there's going to be a confirmation bias around these qualities. You'll probably have to overcompensate. You have to demonstrate that you're low-maintenance, unentitled, attentive to details, can think of others, and can take criticism."

We then unpacked and discussed the principles of the VFA credo, which are:

My career is a choice that indicates my values.

There is no courage without risk.

I believe that actions are the proper measure of one's accomplishments.

I will create value for myself and others.

I will act with integrity in all things.

This credo is the heart of what we have created with Venture for America—an army of builders with a sense of purpose. It isn't enough for Venture Fellows to be smart, action-oriented, competent, and productive; there are a lot of bright people out there. They also need to be trustworthy and driven to create value if they are going to give rise to quality organizations.

We had a wide-ranging discussion about how the Fellows

genuinely felt about these principles, and to what extent. I was glad to find that they had already imagined themselves in the same way—they'd already opted in and chosen a path less traveled, in most cases turning down much more money to do so.

The plan was to whip the Fellows into shape and give them skills and perspective for when they started their jobs. Trainers from McKinsey and Company, Brown University, Cambridge Leadership Associates, and Manhattan Prep, as well as entrepreneurs and investors like David Tisch, spent days with us. David Rose, the CEO of the startup financing platform Gust, laid out the facts on how most new businesses get financed (through friends, family members, and angel investors). The design firm IDEO had the Fellows head into Providence for a day to find a problem and design a solution. Charlie Kroll gave a candid account of his experience building Andera, which had raised $20 million in financing and then acquired another company on the West Coast. Bernie Sucher and other board members visited and spoke. We brought the Fellows to Betaspring, the Providence-based startup accelerator, so they could commune with local startups. We started each morning at 9:00 a.m. and enforced a dress code, in part because we wanted to replicate some aspects of the training one would receive at a professional services firm.

We had a competition during which we asked teams of Fellows to raise as much money as they could for charity for several weeks using the crowdfunded apparel platform Teespring. The winning team raised more than $5,000 for WaterFire Providence by partnering with a local festival and even opening a booth and selling T-shirts at the event one weekend. We had another competition in which the Fellows were tasked with reimagining and redesigning VFA's website and then coding a working version within three days.

As part of each round, we rated each team's performance and published standings. We also had the Fellows provide feedback to each other and discuss individual performance after each challenge. We urged them to be as forthright as possible to make it as informative and honest as it could be. Everyone switched teams a couple of times so they could get a sense of how various people worked and experience different team dynamics. It was important that the Fellows emerge with a sense of how different behaviors might be received in the workplace so that they could become more effective team players.

Training camp was intense but fun. Official hours were from 9:00 a.m. to 6:00 p.m., but each night saw groups working furiously on challenges, listening to a speaker, or attending a dinner or event. On Friday nights, some of the Fellows would gather together to play basketball at the local YMCA or high school. We had an offsite trip to Newport, a couple of barbecues, and a Fellow talent show.

One day, I learned that some of the Fellows had taken advantage of a policy's gray area to use the Brown dining halls (for which they had an ID card) during weekend days when they were also being provided a meal allowance. As a result, Venture for America was being double-charged.

On one level this was the kind of thing you'd expect from enterprising twenty-two- or twenty-three-year-olds who'd been living on campus only weeks earlier. On the other hand it was, in essence, the exact opposite of the culture we were trying to build. Our Fellows were meant to be the antidote to their counterparts, who didn't treat institutional resources as "real" money. And if they were to abuse expenses later, at another place of employment, it might have serious consequences.

My plan was to address them as a group and have an open discussion about it. But as the discussion progressed, I became more and more vocal and bent out of shape. I had been the primary fund-raiser for Venture for America, so it really frustrated me that some of the Fellows were playing fast and loose with the organization's resources. I wound up canceling that evening's proceedings to give everyone a chance to reflect (and, in my own case, to cool off).

The next day, the Fellows came back with a collection of small bills that represented more than we could possibly have been overcharged. We didn't accept it, so they used the money to host a picnic for the team the final week. For many, this was an example of issues we'd discussed in theory becoming real. One Fellow, Sam Stites, said to me afterward, "Thank you. This is the first time that anyone's treated me as an adult." They saw how easy the lines were to cross, and how behavior could be shaped by the institutions and people around them. They began the transition from college students to adult professionals with appropriate responsibilities and expectations.

The whole experience was much more profound than I'd imagined for both the Fellows and the team. Before camp I'd thought, I ran an education company for five years—how different could this be? Very different, as it turns out. We got to know each other in a personal light, as we were all living on campus for weeks. It was quite intense. There were times when I thought I must have the strangest job in the world. I joked with the Fellows that if they were a team of athletes, I was one part cheerleader, one part coach, one part past-his-prime athlete, and one part team owner. I'd imagined today's twenty-two-year-olds to be kind of like me circa 1997, but they're wired differently, capable of things I could never do.

The last couple of days of training camp were sentimental, as the Fellows had a farewell party and said good-bye to each other. Only a couple of weeks later they would throw their belongings into cars and suitcases and arrive in Detroit, New Orleans, Providence, Las Vegas, or Cincinnati to begin the hard work of helping businesses expand and succeed. Mike Mayer became the CEO's chief of staff at Federated Sample, Patrick Comer's tech startup in New Orleans. Kathy Cheng became the business analyst at Doodle Home, a platform for interior designers based in Detroit founded by Jennifer Gilbert. Andy Chatham became a lieutenant at Work in Progress, a startup cooperative workspace venture in Las Vegas funded by Tony Hsieh, CEO of Zappos. And on and on it went.

I went on the road and visited the Fellows that August. I took them out to dinner, saw where they lived and, in many cases, visited where they worked. It was humbling. Many of them were in cities they could never have imagined being in only months earlier—there were twelve in Detroit alone. And they were there doing what they were doing because of an idea I'd had. I felt like a parent in that I knew we would do all we could, but their success was going to be up to them.

You might be curious about how they're doing. Here are firsthand accounts from Mike, Kathy, Andy, Ethan, and Max about their first year in the field:

MICHAEL MAYER *(2012 Venture Fellow in New Orleans)*

After I graduated from Wharton, there was a shared certainty among my class—we'd all end up in New York working in investment banking or consulting. Of course, I knew there were some who deviated from this path but didn't really know who they were or how they did it. The thought of going anywhere else after college didn't exist in my head—partly because I didn't know what other options existed and partly because I was initially comfortable following the herd to the Big Apple.

Needless to say, I could never have predicted I'd be in New Orleans working at a tech startup. New Orleans is an extremely special place—and, no, not (just) because of Bourbon Street or deep-fried oyster po'boys. Out of Katrina's destruction in 2005 came a focused and fiery belief that New Orleans and its people can reclaim new glory. Katrina forced the city to reevaluate what New Orleans represents and what it can become. Now it is one of the fastest-growing and most interesting startup cities because we've had to reboot everything: education, shipping, advanced manufacturing, media, and, of course, fast-growing technology startups.

My experience in New Orleans has focused on two of these "reboots"—fast-growing technology startups and education. Since August 2012, I've been on the front lines of the hottest tech startup in New Orleans, Federated Sample, which builds technology to automate and simplify market research. I didn't join FED because I was passionate about market research but because it successfully disrupts an industry plagued by reluctance to change and inefficiency. On my first day, CEO Patrick Comer told me, "It's not about *if* we are going to explode, it's about *when*." Three months later, I witnessed two of the top five market research firms transition all of their surveys onto our platform, Fulcrum. Patrick came out of his office after one of the last major wins of 2012 and rejoiced. "We still have a long way to go, but we're growing fast and we've made a market." Seeing this happen as an employee is remarkable. Seeing it happen from the perspective of the CEO is transformative. My role as chief of staff puts me inside the CEO's office, literally, and gives me executive-level exposure I never would have received had I not joined Venture for America. What I've learned from Patrick and at Federated Sample will influence the way I view running a business and how I make decisions as a CEO in the future.

Another core component of VFA is community engagement and development. If I'd just wanted to work for a startup after college, I could have gone to San Francisco or New York City. Through VFA, I've gotten the resources, support, and flexibility to get involved and help solve problems in a sector that I'm passionate about. With three other VFA Fellows and mentored by Jeff Weiner, I cofounded Startup Effect (@startup_effect), an enrichment program for middle school students in transitioning US cities to gain confidence and skills through action-oriented entrepreneurial activities and challenges. We bring real businesses into the classroom to pose challenges for our students, who work together in teams to ideate and come up with creative solutions. The response has been overwhelming. Most important, the students are having a blast and learning. Something we hear a lot in the classroom is how "business people are just like you and me." Our students are getting exactly what we set out to give them: exposure and confidence. They realize that running a business or working in the real world is not such a far-off dream. If they work hard and dream big, anything is possible. Additionally, the teachers, principals, local businesses, and the community all see the impact we are making and are extremely excited by where Startup Effect is headed.

All of these experiences I've had in New Orleans would not be as powerful without the network of VFA Fellows at my side. From the group in New Orleans to all those around the country, we are a close-knit group of like-minded individuals always willing to support each other to grow and succeed. And for that more than anything else, I am very proud to call myself a 2012 VFA Fellow.

KATHY CHENG *(2012 Venture Fellow in Detroit)*

When I was growing up, everyone told me to work hard so that I could get into the best colleges and universities in the country. They told me that once I graduated from one of these top-tier schools the world would be open to me. So I aspired, and I got into MIT, arguably one of the best universities for science and technology in the world. However, when those daunting junior and senior years rolled around, when it came time to seriously consider what I wanted to do after graduation, I felt none of that freedom, none of that empowerment. Instead, I felt locked into a choice few "successful" career paths, and for me those manifested as finance and consulting. When the time came to decide on Venture for

America, it was actually not an easy decision for me to make given the confines of traditional success that I had gotten so used to. That being said, it wasn't until I accepted, and whole-heartedly committed to wherever VFA would take me, that I found that elusive sense of empowerment.

VFA took me to Detroit, a city that represented such a sharp veer off the beaten path for me that I was in essence forced to forge my own, one more eccentric and dynamic than I could have otherwise anticipated. Detroit is not ex-actly a glamorous metropolitan center, and, coming from an urban planning background, I found elements of it that were very difficult to adjust to—the lack of walkability, urban den-sity, and public transportation, to name a few. It is certainly not one of the default cities that college graduates would find themselves gravitating toward. What this allowed for, though, was an interesting self-selection in which people who chose to move to Detroit wanted to be here for a reason, thereby creating this engaging community of people who re-ally cared about the city. On the ground, you could almost feel this anxious energy around you as you saw a city with so much need and yet so much potential. The longer you were here, the antsier you became to do something about it.

In terms of my formal employment, I am working for a company called Doodle Home, a virtual studio for interior designers that aims to manage the tasks that interrupt the creative process. For a first job out of college, I couldn't have asked for a better experience. The company represented this intersection of business, technology, and creativity that I was really interested in, and my somewhat vague role as a business analyst allowed me to gain exposure into just about every aspect of the company. As what I was doing adapted to the company's varying needs, I had a chance to explore everything from product development to web analytics, marketing, customer service, usability, and more. The breadth of experience allowed me to see what I enjoyed and perhaps, just as important, what I didn't enjoy. To my surprise and certainly to that of my parents, what I discovered was that while the world of technology was interesting to me, it wasn't quite what I was passionate about. And for me, I needed passion to be at the center of what I was doing.

In the end, it was not the industry of interior design that I found the most captivating; it was the concept. What I found myself continually going back to is how design can activate a space, how I can craft an experience that can inspire creativity, community, and innovation. Suddenly dreams such as opening up my own coffee shop and incubator space or starting a food truck, dreams that were always more of an idyllic vision than a viable option, became real solutions to real problems that I wanted to address in the city. And in fact, it was the non-technical, more traditionally brick-and-mortar ideas that inspired me the most. When I look around Detroit, what drives me is not the need to create technology but the need to activate the many spaces here that are longing for engagement, for a renewed purpose. And what I've come to appreciate the most is that when I have lofty ideas like these, I am no longer afraid to pursue them. Sure, there might be doubts, there might be things that I have no idea how to tackle, but in those moments I can now easily think of three people in the city that I could reach out to who will help me figure it out or connect me to those who can. If there's anything that I can take away from my experiences in VFA, it's the empowerment to craft my own path. If there's anything that I have to be grateful for, it's the supportive community of passionate and motivated people in Detroit who can help me see that path through.

ANDY CHATHAM *(2012 Venture Fellow in Las Vegas)*

Within a week of arriving in Vegas, I could tell I was in the right place. I was immediately working alongside the people who were making decisions and driving change in the world.

My boss, Zach Ware, led the campus development team for Zappos and was starting his own company with two other cofounders. I would come into the office every day not knowing what to expect or even what I would be working on.

By sitting in on countless meetings and listening, I quickly figured out how to contribute and make the lives of those I worked with easier. The team I work on here epitomizes the leadership philosophy preached by Tony Hsieh—Zappos CEO and Downtown Project founder. My colleagues were all friends and would ignore job titles and organizational structure to help each other out and get things done. By embracing this mentality I was able to take on a lot of responsibility early on.

A reality check moment was when I found myself sitting around a table with engineers, architects, and project managers twice my age making decisions on things I had not known existed six months ago. Had I gone the traditional route, I would have spent three to five years within a mature company getting nowhere near the level of responsibility that I had within weeks in Downtown Vegas.

A few months after I started, the next big opportunity came down from Tony to my boss. Tony had been thinking about a plan to fix transportation downtown, and decided it was time to pull the trigger on an investment to make it happen. I spent the next month modeling out a vehicle sharing company that would provide access to everything from bikes to $85,000 Tesla Model S cars. I worked with Zach to summarize and pitch the program, and was eventually given the lead on implementing the early steps and hiring the team to build the product.

Shortly afterward, I found myself sitting across the table from the director of engineering at Tesla, talking about how a company that didn't exist two weeks earlier was going to change transportation for a significant portion of a large city (and the world, after that). The next week I was sitting down with insurance brokers figuring out how to cobble together policies for such an operationally unique program. The week after that I was watching the first $3 million in investment transfer into a company of which I was the only employee.

When I was asked to write this, I said, "Man, the essay will change, depending on what day it is." My story is still being written and rewritten all the time. All I know is that I took a risk and wound up exactly where I wanted to be, in an environment where people are trying to get big things done at an accelerated pace without regard to the status quo.

ETHAN CARLSON *(2012 Venture Fellow in Providence)*

"We might just make it through and have a chance to change the world," she said to me on the three-and-a-half-hour drive back from a potential customer's house. She didn't say we might have a chance to make a lot of money, to maximize shareholder value, or to prove a point. Those things were ancillary. The company didn't exist to make a flash and hope for a big, quick exit, but to make a substantive change in the way the world operated. My boss recognized that fulfillment lay in the creation of real value, something that I've been struggling to learn for most of my adult life.

The company I work at, VCharge Energy, based in Providence, Rhode Island, develops software and hardware that allow certain types of electrical load to interact with the grid in a highly efficient and automated way. This replaces the current blind, one-sided electricity market with a virtual, automated, two-sided one. Market actors can respond to the needs and abilities of each other within the constraints of performing their core function. We are able to give our equipment to consumers for virtually nothing, as well as pass on significant savings to them on their electrical bills, while making money on the back end by taking advantage of the market inefficiencies.

It seems strange now, but two years ago I didn't know this (working at VCharge, or somewhere like VCharge) was what I wanted. My perceptions about what I might or might not want for my career revolved around social expectations rather than intrinsic motivation. I could go to grad school, because then people would think I was smart, or I could join the Peace Corps, so people would think I was caring, or I could be a consultant in Boston or New York, for no other reason than the Yale community seemed to find that path attractive.

Fortunately for me, VFA tricked me into something else. I was told the fellowship would offer the credentialing that I would get other places and, more implicitly, that the "for America" in the name would lend the social credibility and even moral high ground I thought I wanted. I wouldn't live in Boston or New York, but I would be navigating one of these unconventional cities alongside other bright, young, sociable Fellows. Besides, who can't get behind job creation in cities with high unemployment? And startups are supposed to be fun anyway, right?

Those things have all been true, to some extent or another, but the reality has been much, much better. Every day, I get to come into work and collaborate with a small team of people whom I respect highly and who are incredibly brilliant and passionate about what we're trying to accomplish. The work is often engaging and interesting, but it is always meaningful, and I see my creative output reflected in the operations of the company and the lives of our customers. Perhaps most important, the mission of the company feels meaningful. That x factor is indescribable, but its presence or absence can make all the difference.

The dynamic at VCharge is not dissimilar from what is happening in Providence right now. The Creative Capital has been living up to its name, supporting an impressive number of startups and small businesses. The local business incubator, Betaspring, has more applications than it can handle for its biannual class of early-stage companies that facilitate a vibrant and extremely high caliber community of entrepreneurs. The community recognizes its own faults, but is actively working, energetically and with a real sense of fraternity, to solve the issues and move forward.

Over the time of my fellowship I've learned to recognize the value that is present, by necessity, in early-stage companies that are scrapping through whatever insurmountable challenge the day brings—the value in communities that, lacking the high talent density or attention of some other places, turn to investment and community building to create opportunity. It's not something that our society always holds up or makes visible, and certainly not something that our youth are trained to see. But I couldn't be happier that as I learn to appreciate that value I also get to be immersed in it.

MAX NUSSENBAUM *(2012 Venture Fellow in Detroit)*

"So," the woman says to me, "are you going to get a gun?"

It's April of last year, and I've just told someone's mother that I'm headed to Detroit after graduation, to work for a startup as part of Venture for America's inaugural class. Her response isn't exactly typical—no one else suggests that I arm myself—but it's close. One friend jokes that the only item in the *New York Times* article "36 Hours in Detroit" was "Get the hell out of Detroit." Another predicts that my future is going to be like the film *8 Mile*, but with less sex. I talk to a guy who's spending his next year volunteering in a Nigerian slum, and he asks me why I'd ever move somewhere as downtrodden as Detroit. Everyone makes the same dismayed face, asks the same incredulous question: "Why would you go . . . there?"

And "there" wasn't just Detroit. At Wesleyan, my alma mater—like at most elite schools—"there" was anywhere that wasn't a select handful of high-profile cities: the Bostons and New Yorks, the DCs and LAs. We were a cohort raised with tunnel vision, a graduating class that couldn't find Ohio on a map and thought Oklahoma City was an oxymoron. Don't get me wrong, I was more than guilty of this myself: I heard Venture for America talk about underserved parts of the country and my first thought was Queens—you know, since everyone was moving to Brooklyn.

But somehow I was convinced, or if I wasn't entirely convinced I was at least impulsive enough to make the move anyway. I came to Detroit. And I knew I was in the right place.

Much has been made of the extraordinary degree of independence and responsibility that you have at a startup, even as a fresh-faced graduate with your suit still tequila-stained from that one time you wore it to a Halloween party. You can matter at a startup in a way you can't at a big company—not unless you spend years slaving your way up the PowerPoint hierarchy. But less has been said about how the same calculus applies to cities, about how in some cities it's possible to have an impact from the moment you step off the plane.

Detroit is one of those cities. Detroit craves people. And because of that, you can matter the minute you move here.

When you get to Detroit, the city screams at you to do something. It doesn't matter what—just do something. This message is embedded in the feel of the city: in the wide, radial streets, where hipster bicyclists cross paths with 1970s Pontiacs, and in the rotting buildings, post-apocalyptic in their disintegration, that cry out to be rebuilt into something amazing. And it's made even more pressing by the practical opportunities: the abandoned properties that can be bought for a month's rent and the cops who won't stop you, or even necessarily notice, if you want to make some street art of questionable legality. It's an amazing feeling to walk down the street, spot a new business opening up, and realize that— partly thanks to the connections I've made through Venture for America and partly thanks to the entrepreneurial community's interconnectedness—I'm only a few phone calls away from the person starting that business.

Detroit's very into the idea that it hustles hard, but in some ways "Detroit Hustles Harder" is a wholly inaccurate slogan for the city. The point is that it's easier to get your ideas off the ground here than it is in a lot of other places, that the city's rebirth is just a bunch of people's crazy ideas somehow becoming reality. Detroiters are building their city together, from the new transplants lured like I was to the former suburbanites returning from their exile to those who've been here all along, refusing to give in to the weight of the outside world's preconceptions. And it's working. In the six months I've been here I've seen ramshackle high-rises transformed into fussy coffee shops and luxury apartments, the crowds at community fund-raiser Detroit SOUP triple, and NBC swoop in with cameras and stage lights when not long ago we were all breathing into our palms in a heatless building littered with unattached toilets. (Seriously—the organizers had borrowed a warehouse full of old plumbing fixtures.)

People from outside still look at me strangely when I tell them I moved to Detroit. "There's not much in Detroit, is there?" they ask. They don't get that that's the point. I moved to Detroit because the city is full of empty spaces, just waiting for me—for us—to fill them up.[*]

---

[*]For more first-person accounts from fellows, see appendix C.

PART FOUR

The Future

14

How to Get Smart People to Build Things

Some books are about someone who's climbed the mountain and then says, "Here's how I did it." You've probably realized that this isn't one of them, that this book is more about identifying a huge problem and the ways in which this problem can be solved.

The early returns from our Venture for America Fellows' months working in New Orleans, Detroit, Cincinnati, Las Vegas, and Providence have been positive. A few have left or switched companies due to a variety of problems and issues, including bad chemistry and a couple of startups running out of money. However, over half of the companies have grown and hired additional employees after a Fellow started. The companies have added approximately 103 new workers in the past year. The Fellows are helping make it happen—80 percent of the companies rate them to be in the top 1 percent or 10 percent of early hires, and some have become indispensable parts of their enterprises.

They're keeping busy too. The nonprofit that Mike Mayer, Billy Schrero, Brentt Baltimore, and Brian Bosche started to teach entrepreneurship to eighth- and ninth-graders in

Detroit and New Orleans, Startup Effect, is up and running in two schools and has raised more than $40,000 to date. Max Nussenbaum, Tim Dingman, Sean Jackson, and Scott Lowe started Rebirth Realty and raised about $20,000 to buy a fore-closed Detroit house and fix it up for future Fellows. Others have begun working on businesses on the side or volunteering in the community as well. Some have begun working on busi-ness ideas to pitch to the Investment Council after their fel-lowship ends. We have another sixty-eight 2013 Fellows in the original five cities, plus Baltimore, Cleveland, and Philadel-phia, who will be hard at work by the time you read this, with one hundred more on the way in 2014. There are hundreds of enterprising young people and promising startups around the country that we will connect and develop in the coming years.

We don't have any illusions. It's not as if training and de-positing a few dozen brilliant young people in Detroit and other cities every year is going to miraculously rejuvenate each region. They're big communities, and the companies are small. There will be problematic fits. Some Fellows will leave or change environments. Many of the businesses they're working at will fail to progress or collapse entirely. Many of the Fellows will move on after a couple of years to other cit-ies and opportunities, hopefully equipped with a newfound sense of how to build something. Some will go to graduate school, perhaps to return to early-stage companies later.

But let's allow ourselves to imagine that after two years of working at a startup or growth company, the drive to build things gets into their blood. Mike Mayer, Kathy Cheng, or Scott Lowe wind up following in the footsteps of Charlie Kroll, Jen Medbery, or Walker Williams. Scott Lowe starts a business in

Detroit and receives support from VFA as well as local investors; in the first year, he's looking to build a team. In addition to several people in Detroit, ScottCo takes on a couple of other talented hires from Venture for America's upcoming class in 2015. The company expands and grows to a dozen employees. Several years later one of ScottCo's Fellows, having learned a lot from Scott, goes on to start another company and hires a few more people. Research has shown that each high-tech job supports up to five more jobs for people without college educations in the community, bolstering the regional economy.[1] Meanwhile, other Fellows past and present are staying in touch and joining startups around the country, serving as managers or early team members, and these companies also expand. Finally, their friends and classmates see what's possible and start joining teams themselves.

That's how we give rise to the virtuous cycle of job creation and innovation. We seed an environment with both human capital and financial capital and we engage for years. We make it so that building things is the valued path for our top graduates around the country.

There is no quick solution. We have an economy to rebuild and a culture to restore. Hundreds of promising growth companies exist around the country, and thousands of young people who want to help build them. If we build a bridge to connect these two groups, we will unlock an unimaginable amount of potential energy. We're asking a lot of Scott, Tim, Mike, Kathy, and the other Fellows as well as the hundreds that will follow them. But they're embracing the challenge with all of their minds, bodies, and hearts. I hope that you'll join me in doing everything possible to see that they have a chance to succeed.

Leadership matters. We have to show our young people

what is possible and support their training and development in those directions. Why would we make it so easy to become what we don't need while making it so hard to become that which we need most? We have to make it as easy and obvious to be an entrepreneur or team member at an early-stage growth company as it presently is to become a lawyer, banker, doctor, or consultant. We should invest in giving rise to a set of builders who will address the needs of our age.

I'm not saying that everyone should start a company or that everyone should join a startup. That's unrealistic and simplistic. But we should acknowledge that massive forces—and tens of millions of dollars of resources each year—are put into channeling our talent in very specific directions. If we do nothing, what our young people do will continue to be the direct and predictable result of the industries, firms, and institutions that have the necessary resources to recruit and present a ready pathway.

This is not something that any one entity can address alone. It would take an enormous set of counterweights to balance the scales. Through my experiences, I've identified a way forward—policy goals that, if achieved, would have a profound impact on our economy as well as the character and fulfillment of our young people.

Introduce human capital allocation as a policy goal.
Right now, the primary human capital policy focus is on education, which is phenomenally important. But what people do with their education is equally important. We should acknowledge that some industries, activities, and sectors are good for our growth and long-term prospects. We should set human capital allocation goals for startups, growth compa-

nies, and innovation the same way we do the number of science, technology, engineering, and mathematics graduates or average standardized test scores. We should embrace the language of value creation and reward those who train and direct people to build and develop our economic frontier. At a minimum, we should start publishing statistics on where our talent is going each year. As a starting point the data from this book (detailed in appendix F) regarding the paths chosen by national university graduates will be available at http://www.smartpeopleshouldbuildthings.com and will be updated each year based on publicly available data.

Encourage professional services firms to tailor their recruitment.

It's in firms' own best interests to more carefully hire people who will stick around. First, turnover is costly. Second, your culture is stronger if people join you because of a genuine alignment with what you do. Third, in the long term, professional services firms need thriving growth companies to be prosperous themselves. Goldman Sachs, often a leader in its industry, recently did away with its two-year analyst program for graduates straight out of college because it found it wasn't an effective funnel for talent into the firm—even analysts they wanted to retain after the two years were departing for private equity firms, hedge funds, or business school. For most firms, entry-level employees are a loss leader. At my law firm, attorneys weren't moneymakers for the firm until our third year, when our billing rates rose and we were more productive. The attrition rate at top consulting firms is 20–30 percent per year, a clear sign that their strategy of "hire every smart person in sight" has a significant downside. Professional services firms should examine both their attrition and retention rates and install significant up-front processes to identify committed hires with a higher probability of being a long-term cultural fit (at a minimum, consultants should really like to travel).

Make growth companies a distinct category for university career services and invest resources to level the playing field for smaller firms.

University career services offices should invest in identifying diverse opportunities with growth companies around the country. Each career services office should have a growth company liaison who reaches out to small and midsize growth companies to determine their hiring needs. Career services offices should be evaluated based on the breadth and nature of opportunities that are promoted to students. Universities should also pursue and publish detailed metrics on what their alumni are doing years after graduation—they already keep track of them for development purposes. There should be "new firm" and "growth company" categories for companies less than five years old. You improve what you measure. Ideally, national universities would pool resources to invest in an agency that would act as a clearinghouse and ensure that a level playing field exists between firms large and small. Our national universities are publicly funded and supported; at a minimum their tax-exempt status saves them hundreds of millions of dollars per year. What their graduates do should be regarded as an official goal and a public policy concern.

Provide scholarships and loan forgiveness for graduates heading to growth companies.

Universities and MBA programs ought to fund postgraduate scholarships for and forgive the loans of any honors graduate who starts or joins a qualifying early-stage business upon graduation. We should do whatever we can to encourage not just starting a company but joining a recently founded one. Early startup hires often become the next generation of executives and founders, and any entrepreneur will tell you that a strong early team is a crucial element to getting a business off the ground. Companies and regional entities could assist in funding these scholarships to benefit local enterprises. For example, Procter and Gamble could offer a scholarship to pay back loans for honors students who join a Cincinnati-based startup.

Enforce transparency and better financial data for educational institutions.

Colleges, law schools, business schools, culinary schools, art schools, vocational schools, and all other educational institutions should provide easy-to-understand data to applicants concerning employment prospects, average indebtedness, and an average loan payment the student should expect per month based upon prevailing interest rates and the usual repayment period. Employment data should be audited to include only those jobs that require the respective degree and should be signed by the head of the institution— with civil and regulatory penalties for any misrepresentation. The head of every educational institution should be required to meet each year with a randomly selected group of recent alumni to get a sense of their experiences and concerns. Young people are making life-altering decisions based upon incomplete and unclear information. If we want today's graduates to take risks and build new businesses, we can't have them systemically graduating with tens of thousands in debt that will take years to pay off in the best of circumstances. Ideally, transparency, clear communication, and more rigorous administration of public loan availability will engender more rational education decisions, lower tuition rates, and lower levels of indebtedness over time.

Present builders as role models.

Universities, media companies, and public figures should promote startup entrepreneurs as role models and invite them to tell their stories. Leaders such as Brian Balasia of Digerati in Detroit, Lucinda Duncalfe of Real Food Works in Philadelphia, and Miles Lasater of Higher One in New Haven, Connecticut, are all inspirational figures who have created dozens of jobs around the country. Miles Lasater stayed in New Haven after graduating from Yale to build a company that helped schools process student payments. His company went public in 2010 and now employs over five hundred people in its New Haven headquarters and elsewhere. There are builders like Miles in every region. Every university should have an "entrepreneurship hour" like the University of Michigan has, when an experienced entrepreneur comes and speaks to hundreds of students. An unheralded team member should also come in to talk about what it's like being the fifth person on the team. Campus newspapers should regularly profile appropriate alumni and ask them how they got where they are. Plato wrote that "What is honored in a country is cultivated there." Role models and narratives are important.

Include a path and values discussion in college and embrace the co-op or gap year.

At many schools and universities, the first time students hear anyone talking about what they should do with their lives is during their commencement speech on graduation day. There should be some guidance and values imparted to our young people beyond simple achievement, status, or even intellectual exploration. Parents and schools should encourage students to take a year off either before or during college to get some real-world exposure and experience, ideally working in different environments through a co-op program like the one at Northeastern University. I meet seniors in college all the time, and they have a very vague idea of what roles are available to them beyond the obvious ones and little sense of how the economy functions. Universities should invest in helping their students understand what different options look like and what they represent. They should even feel free to advocate. It's not enough anymore to let the market do its thing; there's a war for talent under way, and sitting on the sidelines is no way to influence its outcome.

Improve and invest in entrepreneurship education.

Entrepreneurship education should become more action-oriented and real-world driven. One student at Columbia said to me, "All we see around here are successful entrepreneurs who have made it and have happy endings. What about the others?" At present, the study of entrepreneurship is abstract and often ends upon graduation, when it's time to get a "real job." Moreover, the courses are generally regarded as less demanding and attractive to employers than other disciplines like physics or finance. Entrepreneurship course work should consist of actions undertaken for real organizations and should involve real money and selling things. Entrepreneurship programs should be producing real businesses and contributors each year, if only on a small scale. Most business building is not about a clever idea but about high-level and consistent execution.

Enlist entrepreneurs as mentors.

Universities, business schools, and even law schools and medical schools should develop a roster of alumni entrepreneurs who are willing to speak, give advice, or even take on paid apprentices. Interested applicants should compete via an application process in order to qualify, followed by individual interviews to determine fit. Many veteran entrepreneurs would enjoy having an ambitious young person from their school around, and most entrepreneurs believe that the best training is to work alongside a more experienced veteran. The Yale Entrepreneurial Institute is an example of a successful university effort to enlist experienced entrepreneurs as mentors for current students.

Make accelerators and incubators more accessible.

It's difficult to devise a business plan and develop a company that is accepted by an accelerator that then goes on to raise additional funding. The bar is way too high for most recent graduates; most accelerators that take in startup founders and help them get off the ground have acceptance rates as low as 1–3 percent. To make opportunities more accessible, accelerators and incubators should maintain a selective database of students and recent graduates, perhaps from local universities, who are willing to act as volunteer unpaid labor or interns for their companies after the accelerator program is over. Startups would select workers from the talent bench. Over time, graduates would get some experience and wind up connected to any emerging companies.

Form and expand regional innovation hubs.

Organizations such as CincyTech, the Brandery, and Cintrifuse in Cincinnati; Idea Village in New Orleans; JumpStart in Cleveland; Betaspring in Providence; and TEDCO in Columbia, Maryland, have each served as an invaluable launch pad for a host of businesses by providing capital, advice, inexpensive real estate, and a place to network. Government officials and leaders, community foundations, economic development corporations, universities, chambers of commerce, and local enterprises should support existing innovation hubs or create new hubs to attract young companies or encourage the building of new ones.

Entrepreneurs should reach back.

Successful entrepreneurs are often very focused on their current venture or latest interest—it's one of their defining traits. Their early career quickly recedes into the rearview mirror, and it's natural to let others address the concerns of recent graduates. Yet the entrepreneurs themselves remain the best equipped to supply the insight, perspective, and resources others need to follow in their footsteps. Many could do more to share their stories, mentor and fund up-and-comers, and make sure that others understand the process from inside the trenches. Kevin Plank of Under Armour is a prominent example of an entrepreneur who has done an outstanding job giving back in order to inspire others; Kevin has funded and mentored numerous entrepreneurs in addition to founding and leading a Fortune 1000 apparel company in Baltimore. Dan Gilbert, Tony Hsieh, Steve and Jean Case, Josh Kopelman, Arianna Huffington, and other entrepreneurs—many less famous—are cut from the same cloth in that they give their time and resources to cultivate the next generation. We need more like them.

Support risk-takers you know.
Each of us knows people who go out there on a limb. Perhaps your son, having just graduated from college, is working for a new company you've never heard of, and you'd prefer that he did something a bit more secure. Or you have a friend who is trying to start a new organization or gather people together for a cause or other activity. It's tempting to try and talk sense into—or, more likely, ignore—your friend. It's true that things might not work out. But open up and be supportive; know that he will learn from these experiences. Show up to something. He'll show up to your thing too, and the world will be a better place for it.

Most policy lists like this one go nowhere. Let's make this one an exception.

Finally, we need to provide a direct, concrete, and actionable path that motivated graduates can take to learn and develop what it takes to build and grow a value-creating business. Entrepreneurship is like most things—you tend to get better at it over time. The toughest part is getting started. We have to make it easier to get started as a builder.

Imagine a country where the same body of talent that is currently heading to Wall Street and professional services was instead going to startups and growth companies around the country. How long would that take to impact the rate of job growth and innovation?

We can transform the economy and renew our culture to include value creation, risk and reward, and the common good. We can prepare a critical mass of our best and brightest to become a network of builders and job creators. But our success or failure will be determined not by the merit of the idea but by our ability to recruit top college graduates who want to learn to build businesses, identify promising startups and growth companies around the country, and support training, placement, and programming for hundreds of talented young people each year. If you feel this is a cause worth supporting, please visit http://www .ventureforamerica.org. You can see how the story goes and become a part of it in real time. Let's solve this problem together. If we do, we'll solve a lot of other problems at the same time. We've got a plumbing problem and we need a new pipe.

I'll close with an excerpt from Scott Lowe's application essay to Venture for America. Scott had a near-perfect grade point average in engineering physics at the University of Oklahoma and now works at Chalkfly, an e-commerce startup in Detroit, while rehabbing a foreclosed house for Fellows to live in:

> For the past twenty-one years I've struggled to find meaning in life, and it wasn't until I truly began considering career paths that I came to the realization that life is not about making money. The Dalai Lama, when asked what surprised him most about humanity, wisely responded, "Man, because he sacrifices his health in order to make money.

Then he sacrifices money to recuperate his health. And then he is so anxious about the future that he does not enjoy the present; the result being that he does not live in the present or the future; he lives as if he is never going to die, and then dies having never really lived." This quote changed my life.

Just months ago, I was on track toward becoming a quant; in fact, my senior capstone research is centered around financial mathematics: studying information cascades in FOREX markets using Fokker-Plank equations, researching several econophysics models, including the statistical treatment of money, wealth, and income, and learning traditional financial mathematics, including option pricing theory, via the Black-Scholes equation. While I enjoy the work because of my love of mathematics, I luckily realized that this career path was simply designed to exploit inefficiencies in markets in order to extract profits from others. This financial realm known as trading is a zero-sum game where for every dollar you make, someone else loses a dollar, and I know I'm not destined to become such an obvious parasite on society. I only aspire to lead a meaningful, impactful life where I can apply my skills as an extremely analytical individual toward the benefit of humanity. I'm constantly in awe of what we have achieved as a species, but I'm also fully aware that there are plenty of problems left to tackle from government, to education, to corporate America. I only hope I get the opportunity to work toward solutions for these problems.

Our young people desperately want the chance to participate in and lead our nation's economic and cultural revival. They're up for the challenges that they're going to inherit. It only remains for us to present the opportunity.

Acknowledgments

I run a nonprofit—there are hundreds of people I should thank, too many to count here.

Thank you to Eileen Lee, Mike Tarullo, Megan Hurlburt, Eddie Shiomi, Lauren Gill, Liz Deogracias, Jason Tarre, Seon-hye Moon, Amy Nelson, Jackie Miller, Zeve Sanderson, Leandra Elberger, Joe Guy, Domenic Merolla, and the rest of the Venture for America team. You are building the engine of human capital transformation that will serve as one of the defining projects of our time. (I know you all will go on to do some other amazing things, so I can't say this is going to be the definitive high for you!)

Thank you to Charlie Kroll, Bernie Sucher, Cameron Breitner, Darren MacDonald, John Delbridge, Sy Jacobs, Michael Kahan, Dan Rosenthal, LeRoy Kim, Charlie Penner, Eric Cantor, Peter Ezersky, Jeremy Shinewald, Robin Chan, Jay Bockhaus, Andy Parker, Princess Khaliya, Dan Porter, Andy Weissman, Dave Tisch, Marty Halbfinger, Brandon Pollak, Alisa Volkman, Gary Horowitz, Alison Lindland, Jason van Itallie, Dan Kelley, Field Price, Dave Gilboa, Cariann

Chan, Guillermo Silberman, Matt Wisdom, Chip Hazard, Gary Chou, Eric Bahn, Katherine Farley, Miles Lasater, Josh Linkner, David Lee, Samer Hamadeh, Mike Borofsky, Stuart Schultz, Tina Imm, and everyone else for joining the boards of a fledgling little nonprofit and helping make it real.

Thank you to Fred Dust and IDEO, Sanjay Kalavar and McKinsey, Miika Grady, Mana Behbin, Marian Salzman and Havas PR, Fiona and Matt Singer, Julie Covello, Greg and So-phia Gushee, Mark Opler, Sofija Jovic, Emilian Djindic, Lisa Gruber, Richard Dukas, Rob Tsai, Anthony Hemsey, Barbara Tannenbaum, Jack Basavaiah, Simpson Thacher and Bart-lett, Fumi Osode, and everyone else who worked or provided things for free when we weren't paying for things.

Thank you, Zeke, for the opportunity and for years of partnership.

Thank you to Chris Ryan, Dan Gonzalez, Eric Cabal-lero, Sam Edla, Peter Lee, Ronit Reinhard, Danielle Di-Ciaccio, Noah Teitelbaum, Dave Mahler, Evyn Williams, Dan McNaney, Jessie Trujillo, Kimberly Moy, Taylor Dearr, Brie Truesdell, Jessica Eliav, Beretzi Garcia, and everyone else at Manhattan Prep for building a great organization.

Thank you to Mat Farkash and Zeev Klein for helping us spread the word to the right people, and to Lori Feinsil-ver, Jamie Sears, Bob McCann, Shannon Schuyler, Rebecca Kaplan, Lane Jost, Kerry Sullivan, Kristy Tesky, Wynne Lum, Amy Stursberg, Tony Tolentino, Debbie Goldfarb, Scott Roen, Elisabeth Yarbrough, Michelle Burschtin, Neil Steinberg, Adrian Bonet, Eric Avner, Kathy Merchant, Shi-loh Turner, Robert Embry, Beth Harber, Bhikhaji Maneckji, Zak Pashak, Dalila Wilson-Scott, Lois Backon, Stephen Piazza, Joe Nagle, David Rose, Greg Ho, Nick and Ashley

Sanicola, and Alan Hassenfeld for being the right people.

Thank you to Tony Hsieh, Jeff Weiner, Dan Gilbert, and Arianna Huffington for the confidence and support early on.

Thank you to the Fellows and the young people who have taken on the challenge that Venture for America presents. Our organization wouldn't exist without you; you're why we're here and I'm sure you'll build amazing things in the years to come.

Thank you to everyone who has contributed time and money to bring Venture for America to life. We will do our utmost to have a sustained impact and live up to your commitment.

Thank you to Beppie Huidekoper, Barry Rosenstein, Lauren Zalaznick, Marisa Quinn, Todd Andrews, Jayran Davani, Michael Thorp, and Brown University for providing VFA its first home.

Thank you to the builders throughout the country who do the hard work for uncertain reward, and thanks also to those who help them. You demonstrate what's possible, and it's been a privilege getting to know at least a few of you.

On the book front, Byrd Leavell ran me down and made it happen. Ren Li helped with the research. Hollis Heimbouch, Colleen Lawrie, and many friends and colleagues made suggestions and comments to earlier manuscript versions to help improve the final result.

Occasionally someone asks me why I thought I could do something in the world. For that I'd give full credit to my parents and my brother, Larry.

Thank you, Evelyn, for being the best partner and companion anyone could ask for—building a family with you is my proudest accomplishment.

Christopher, you're too small to read this, but I'm hoping this ends up touching the land you're going to grow up in.

Appendix A: Venture for America Mission Statement and Credo

MISSION:

To revitalize American cities and communities through entrepreneurship.

To enable our best and brightest to create new opportunities for themselves and others.

To restore the culture of achievement to include value creation, risk and reward, and the common good.

IMMEDIATE GOAL:

To help create 100,000 new US jobs by 2025.

Venture for America applicants agree to the following statements as part of their application process:

- I see my professional pursuits and my career as a moral choice that indicates my values.
- I appreciate those who assume personal risks in order to build a company or pursue a common good.

- I believe that actions are the proper measure of one's accomplishments.
- I believe that creating value and opportunities for myself and others is an important aspect of professional success.
- I believe that one's professional conduct is a reflection of personal character, and will always strive to act accordingly.

Venture for America Fellows adopt the following credo:

- My career is a choice that indicates my values.
- There is no courage without risk.
- I believe that actions are the proper measure of one's accomplishments.
- I will create value for myself and others.
- I will act with integrity in all things.

Appendix B: The State of Venture for America

Venture for America has raised approximately $6.5 million since 2011 to revitalize American cities and communities through entrepreneurship. In addition to Tony Hsieh's $1 million commitment for Las Vegas, we received a pledge of $1.5 million from Dan Gilbert and Quicken Loans for Detroit and Cleveland* and a $1.2 million multiyear commitment from UBS Americas. Other significant supporters include Jeff Weiner, Reid Hoffman, American Express, the PwC Foundation, the Bank of America Foundation, the Barclays Foundation, the Blackstone Foundation, the Abell Foundation, the Skoll Foundation, IAC, Sy Jacobs, the Rhode Island Foundation, the Carol Ann and Ralph V. Haile, Jr./US Bank Foundation, the Greater Cincinnati Foundation, CVC Capital Partners, the JP Morgan Chase Foundation, the Sarnicola Foundation, and many others. Our budget for 2014 is

---

*I met with Dan in Detroit in mid-2013. I told him how much I admired his work for the city, and that I was there to be his special forces recruiter. Having seen some of the Fellows in action, he understood what we're building with VFA and immediately committed to help.

approximately $3 million with a full-time staff of twelve dedicated employees for Fellow recruitment, selection, training, placement, programming, support, and development.

After reading this book, I hope you feel that these early donors are visionaries that are ahead of the curve. We're incredibly grateful to each of them. They understand that if, as a country, we can activate more of our talent, everyone will benefit.

We had hundreds of applicants again in 2013, and another sixty-eight Fellows are on their way to startups around the country. We're expanding to Baltimore, Cleveland, and Philadelphia, and are looking at Pittsburgh, San Antonio, Kansas City, Oklahoma City, Tulsa, Columbus, and St. Louis, among many other markets. A number of other cities have already reached out to us. It's a big country, and there's a lot of work to do.

Let's put our people to work solving problems, building growth businesses, and creating opportunities for themselves and others. If you'd like to keep up with how we're doing or support VFA, please visit http://www.ventureforamerica.org or follow us on social media. We have the talent—it's just being poorly allocated. Let's solve the problem together.

Appendix C: Accounts from 2012 and 2013 Venture Fellows

Each of the Fellows has a great story. I've included some below, and you can get a sense of all of them at our website.

TIM DINGMAN *(2012 Venture Fellow in Detroit)*

Every weekday, I wake up in my Detroit apartment and drive to my office on the outskirts of town. Attached to the office is what seems like a garage but is actually a wind tunnel. We use the wind tunnel to test our prototype of the wind power generator we're designing at Accio Energy. The generator has no blades or turbines; instead, it uses the motion of charged water droplets to generate electricity. There's a lightbulb attached to the wind tunnel that lights up during testing to prove we're actually generating power.

The environment I'm in now is worlds away from the one I imagined myself in a couple of summers ago. For years, the plan had been simple: get a PhD, become a researcher, discover a breakthrough technology, and save the world. I was in Singapore for a research position and was already on track to get my master's in electrical engineering from Brown, where I'd just finished my bachelor's a month before. By that time, I had already decided the PhD track was not for me. For the previous two years I had run a design conference at Brown and the Rhode Island School of Design (RISD) called "A Better World by Design." I found the experience invigorating and began thinking I might be able to have a more direct, immediate impact on the world outside of the lab.

So there I was, sitting at my laptop in a hostel in Singapore, having moved there for the summer to take a position that I no longer wanted, when I spotted a tweet about a new organization called Venture for America. As soon as I finished scouring VFA's website, I knew I had to be a part of the program. The combination of technology, entrepreneurship, and urban revitalization was exactly what I was looking for. I applied while finishing my master's degree. To my delight, I received an offer, and I accepted on the spot.

Since that fateful day in January 2012, I have experienced an incredible variety of people, places, things, and ideas. The five-week training camp gave me exposure to a wide variety of skills well outside my realm of academic experience. In my job, I have seen the importance of team and culture while honing my engineering skills and working with some talented builders.

The city of Detroit has been a lesson in itself, showing me what a city with nothing to lose can achieve if enough determined citizens put their minds and bodies to work. Organizations like Detroit SOUP, D:hive, and Opportunity Detroit are bringing people and ideas into Detroit at a breakneck pace. Downtown shows new signs of life every time I look out my window. Anchor institutions like Wayne State University and the Detroit Medical Center keep the Midtown neighborhood vital. The rebirth of Motor City is happening before my eyes.

Most important, however, are the people. I've learned a lot from the other Fellows, who are from many different geographic and academic places. They are my better angels, holding me to high standards by holding themselves to the same levels. I lead forty lives by learning from their experiences.

My future is a lot less certain than it used to be, but I find that I'm OK with that. Accio's wind generator may become a breakout success—if it does, I will have contributed to the success of a renewable energy company at the age of twenty-four, which would be something beyond my wildest expectations (and I will probably have saved some birds from whirring blades). Whatever the future holds, I'm confident that I'll be in a position to help build something while using parts of myself that I'd only recently discovered.

JIM KAHMANN *(2012 Venture Fellow in Cincinnati)*

In the fall of 2011, I returned from a summer in Honolulu confronted by an enormous void. That void was my future. It was my senior year at Columbia University, and I had no clue what to fill my future with.

Like the majority of my peers at Columbia, Manhattan's financial behemoths beckoned to me. Working at Bank of America Merrill Lynch the summer before, I was in close proximity to mass layoffs and had witnessed firsthand the enormous financial losses of that August's market slump.

The banking industry was hemorrhaging, but I didn't know where else to turn.

I'll admit that the idea of searching beyond the Hudson River for my future was frightening. I had heard about Venture for America on campus, but had discounted that route as not appropriate for someone like me. One week before the last Venture for America application deadline, I sat down and had a very real conversation with a friend of my grandfather's, Evan Smith, a consultant at Shafer Consulting in Stamford, Connecticut. I entered the meeting hoping I was going to find a cubicle job at his firm. Instead, we had a far-ranging conversation about life and careers. He told me, "If there's any time you're going to take a risk and try to build something, it's right now." Two hours later, I was on the train back to New York City, redefining my future. I didn't need someone to give me a job. I was going to create a job. The void I saw in my future was no longer a liability, but my greatest opportunity.

Many essays and interviews later, I received and promptly accepted an offer from Venture for America. During VFA's summer training camp, my team bombed in the first competition and was thrown into disarray. This loss created a sense of futility and disunity—a void that could only be filled by victory, which at that moment seemed far beyond reach. But this void also presented a great opportunity. We could only do better, so that's exactly what we did. We went the extra mile, took an online competition door to door over the weekend, and finished first by a wide margin in VFA's final group competition. It's a lot of fun being the dark horse.

Now I do business development and sales for OneMore-Pallet, a very small startup company based in Cincinnati.

We're trying to fill a large void in an old industry. Literally, that's what we do every day—develop software to fill otherwise empty space on freight trucks. On average, one-third of the space in every truck on the road runs unused. We think this particular void is worth over $60 million per year. Filling it would be good for the environment too.

The truly ambitious—the frontiersman—braves the void. He seeks it out because it's an opportunity. I joined Venture for America and OneMorePallet looking for wide-open opportunities, and I haven't been disappointed.

EDIE FEINSTEIN *(2012 Venture Fellow in New Orleans)*

I was six years old when my family took its first trip to New Orleans for the Jazz and Heritage Festival. We loved it so much we came back, and over the next few years we became festival regulars, enthusiastic about eating alligator, getting invited to crawfish boils, and hopping between music tents to catch as much as possible.

Venture for America gave me the opportunity to come back to New Orleans as an adult to join a company that is having a real impact on the trajectory of the city's startup ecosystem.

I didn't always dream of working for an educational software company, but I was inspired and impressed by Kickboard's founder and CEO, Jen Medbery, from the first time we spoke on the phone, and I accepted the job without hesitation.

Kickboard has been heralded as one of New Orleans' startup success stories, raising a seed round and more recently a Series A round, not an easy task. The company has also smartly capitalized on the innovative nature of the charter schools here, which are more willing to experiment with education technology than most schools around the country.

Eight months in, I have already learned so much about growing a business and, more specifically, a software company. I was given real responsibility from day one. Very soon after joining I took charge of monitoring and responding to all incoming communication from customers and working on side projects to improve our customer onboarding process, knowledge base, and more. By the time my two years are up I will have seen Kickboard raise venture capital, more than triple the number of employees, and (hopefully) quadruple in revenue.

This is not your typical entry-level, first-year-out-of-college experience.

Bob Dylan once wrote, "New Orleans, unlike a lot of those places you go back to that don't have the magic anymore, still has got it."

I would argue that New Orleans has "got it" now more than ever before, as smart people flock to the city to start businesses and venture capitalists turn their attention here. New Orleans has a special sauce of passionate people, supportive mentors, powerful tax credits, and—perhaps most important—the will to succeed.

Without Venture for America, I may have never thought to look to New Orleans for more than the music and food I loved so much as a kid. Hidden behind the intoxicated spring breakers on Bourbon Street and the beignets at Café du Monde there is an entrepreneurial ecosystem taking shape that I have been lucky to be a part of.

BARRY CONRAD *(2012 Fellow in Las Vegas)*

In school I studied broadcast meteorology. I wanted to be Barry the weatherman.

I'll spare you the details, but I soon realized that the glamorous life of chasing twisters through the plains of Oklahoma wasn't really my calling. And—who am I kidding?—my hair would never cut it on the news.

I started studying business and finance. I had two goals during the confusing years that followed: not to get boxed in, and to be my own boss. Unfortunately, in many ways our collegiate system is set up to place us in a box, ship us off, and not encourage us to explore our entrepreneurial ambitions. Our universities have our best interests at heart; they want us to land a job right out of school, move up the ranks to ensure we have some job security, and eventually write a nice check to their newest scholarship fund for their troubles.

For many this process works great, and our universities provide their best talent with all of the necessary tools to hop on the "success" bandwagon. Their secret weapon is the companies they bring in to recruit said talent. Where I went to school, this was mainly large energy companies and mid-size banks with some smaller-scale consulting firms thrown into the mix. In other areas of the country this would also include more large-scale consulting firms and financial institutions. More broadly, these are the companies that have deep pockets—and boy, can they put on a show.

Let's be honest; most of the time it's an easy sell for a broke college student. I remember being on recruiting trips where I'd roll into a five-star hotel, valet my 1996 Toyota Camry, and order sixty-dollar room service in the morning. I was thinking, "This is the life!" It was like that one time that pretty girl in all my classes finally started to warm up to the idea of us dating. At the time, nothing seemed to be wrong with those situations. In reality, though, she was just trying to get to my best friend, and these big corporations needed me to become something specific in order to fill a role.

It's not really our universities' faults for setting this path before us. For many of our classmates this is a fantastic route to follow, and this is the path they set out on when they entered school. For the entrepreneurs, though, it's our fault if we let the allure of a nice salary and fancy perks draw us away from what we love to do. After all, we've been on a mission to be different our entire lives, so why stop now?

Somewhere in the middle of this recruitment onslaught, the entrepreneur will typically experience what I like to call a "holy cow" moment. I remember mine quite fondly. I was sitting in my room with three massive case study books practicing my profitability question framework responses while my roommate grilled me on the direct and indirect costs of a fictional company. "Holy cow," I thought, "what is the value in doing these exercises? If I continue down this path, when will I be able to get out and do my own thing? Could my time be better spent building a business, maybe learning how to write code or optimize a website for starters?"

The answer to me, and to any entrepreneur, is an obvious and resounding yes. We don't excel at learning a process and repeating it over and over again. We like to take a problem and beat the crap out of it until it works right, and then find another problem and do the same thing. We want to have an impact right now, and if not now, at least soon.

When I heard what Venture for America had to say I

couldn't get enough. VFA really and truly understood me when my university and recruiters didn't have the slightest clue. More than anything, though, the people at VFA didn't seem to have any intention of changing me—they wanted me to become the person I wanted to be.

ZOE CHAVES *(2013 Venture Fellow)*

When I was just five years old, my mother took me to a small private practice in New York City for a routine physical, at which we met a doctor who changed our lives. Upon learning that we were uninsured and living on a family friend's pull-out couch, because my mom didn't have sufficient employment at the time, he did everything he could to help us; he ripped up the check my mother gave him to pay for the exam, and pledged to help me attain a good education, eventually connecting me to the full-ride scholarship that has made my Ivy League education possible. By helping to keep our family stable at a time of vulnerability, my doctor made it possible for my mom to keep climbing the ladder at work, and now she enjoys a great job with a lot of responsibilities and benefits.

So when I first arrived in Providence in 2009 to study at Brown University, I did so with a strong desire to pay my doctor's generosity forward, and effect positive, sustainable change in my new hometown. I joined the Brown chapter of the national nonprofit Health Leads, which mobilizes college students to work with low-income hospital patients. By connecting diabetic patients to food stamps and asthmatic children to mold remediation services, I improved their individual health outcomes and made the case for a more holistic health care system that addresses patients' basic resource needs. Through Health Leads I learned about the tremendous poverty that marks this city.

In 2011 I met a disabled mother who didn't speak English, whose utilities had been shut off that morning for reasons she couldn't understand. I called her service provider and was relieved to learn that her utilities had been cut off accidentally. The man on the phone told me that he would be happy to send someone to restore her services—in three days. I gathered up all the persuasive force inside of me and told him that if the company hadn't made a thoughtless error, her utilities wouldn't have been off at all. I told him that my client relies on a cane to get around and has very young children, and that I would hate for their fall risk to be increased because of the company's mistake. Her services were restored by 6:00 p.m. that day.

It felt like—and was—a huge victory for both my client and me, but I couldn't help but think about what her next steps would be. How long would it be until something like this happened again? How sustainable was yelling at her utilities provider, really? To be really secure, my client needed English-language education and a job that would allow her to make ends meet. Looking back on all the clients I worked with through Health Leads, I realized that getting a job was the only thing that deeply changed my clients' lives and opportunities, and that far too few had been able to achieve that, due to the lack of jobs and job growth in our community. In many ways, I felt that at Health Leads I was finding spare pieces of pie for my clients, while what all of us really needed was to just make the pie bigger.

So I began thinking, "How could one create decent jobs in a community?" I spent my senior year trying to answer this question and concluded that entrepreneurship and growing small businesses was the answer. I resolved to put my energy toward this new goal. After months of searching, I heard about a new program called Venture for America, which seemed like a perfect fit. I wasn't sure if they'd want a non-engineer like me, but I decided to apply. Now I'm set to learn how to build a business alongside some very talented people, and I couldn't be more excited for it.

ASTRID SCHANZ-GARBASSI *(2013 Venture Fellow)*

For my entire child and adolescent life, I've been delighted with what I will call my "story of self." When I introduced myself to strangers I felt a sense of confidence, security, and general satisfaction about my path and my prospects. My choices, my interests, and my plans were all met with acceptance, understanding, and approval. "Mmm, yes," my audience and I mused, "this girl is going someplace." And that affirmation infused enormous confidence in every action, thought, idea, conversation, and challenge I took on.

But when I graduated from Middlebury College in May 2012 with a physics degree, all of that changed.

At some moment or another before walking across the stage to accept my diploma, I decided that I wanted to be an entrepreneur. Specifically, I wanted to launch YouPower, an energy-producing bike room I'd created on my college campus, as a real business. So I started telling that story to myself and to others.

Immediately I sensed a change. Behind the plaster of polite nods and smiles there was a real emptiness in the responses I got. New acquaintances, old friends, and even family members seemed skeptical—if not downright disbelieving—that I would ever succeed. When I enthused to the world that I was an "aspiring entrepreneur," I could tell my listeners were thinking "delusional unemployment" instead. Slowly this attitude infected my own perception of what I was doing, what I was capable of, and where I was going. For the first time, I no longer liked my own story.

This was dangerous. As Tina Seelig writes in her book, *What I Wish I Knew When I Was 20*, "attitude is perhaps the best indicator of what we are capable of accomplishing." I knew that with my current mind-set, I could not accomplish what I hoped to. I needed a better one.

Enter Venture for America. Yes, VFA will give me useful skills, connect me with an invaluable network, and inspire me with information compiled by experienced mentors who are farther along the path I hope to travel. But even before I show up for summer training, VFA has already given me the most incredible tool of all. It's restored my faith in myself and my enthusiasm for entrepreneurship, and given me confidence to pursue this path and the assurance that I'm not doing it alone. When I explain to others how I'll be spending the next two years, my voice oozes with passion. I'm relieved to say that the cynical responses have been replaced with celebratory ones. It's given me my story back.

VFA has given all of its Fellows a way to pursue the typically daunting startup path without forcing them to abandon their "I can" attitudes. Even more than the ability to code, raise funds, or persuade, this is perhaps *the* defining quality that can distinguish a successful entrepreneur from a failed one—or one who never tried at all. If not for Venture for America, I may very well have been the latter.

JIM PLEW *(2013 Venture Fellow)*

For years I was a perfect example of your typical overachieving undergrad. Finance major. Investment banker-to-be. I was driven, capable, and determined to be the best. And I was damn proud of it.

Sound familiar?

That's because I wasn't alone. Like many of my peers, I was relentless in my pursuit of achievement and unwavering in my pursuit of success. And for me, success meant the corner office at a big bank or a Fortune 500 company. Almost every decision I made in the early part of my undergraduate career was shaped by this desire to make it to the top.

So, what's wrong with this picture? Isn't ambition a good thing? I certainly thought so, but with the benefit of hindsight, I can tell you what I was missing.

At the height of my feverish climb toward these glamorous careers, I had a discussion with a graduate admissions adviser about my career path and what I needed to do to get there. As always, I had loads of questions and was determined to walk away with answers to every last one of them. But after some time, the only answer I came away with went something like this: "If you don't love it, don't do it. Everything else will take care of itself."

I'll never forget those words, but I was slightly aggravated upon hearing them at first. Here I was thinking that I had it all figured out and all I needed were a few more concrete answers to reinforce my original assumptions. But what I got only spurred more questions, and most of them were very difficult to answer.

Perhaps the most important question was this: Why did I really select investment banking?

Once I was honest with myself, I discovered that I didn't like the answer. Like most of my peers, I chose investment banking because it was the "thing to do" if you were a smart and ambitious business student; you just followed the rest of your equally aspirational peers into banking or consulting. These are both very challenging and rewarding paths, but so are many other careers. I realized that I had never even stopped to consider my own genuine beliefs and values, and without this self-awareness, I was channeling all of my energy and ambition into a career that wasn't for me. And the worst part is, many of us are.

It's time for my generation to face an ugly truth: life is too short to chase a career you aren't passionate about. And this doesn't apply only to those pursuing investment banking, it applies to everyone.

If you don't love it, don't do it.

So, what do I love? At the core, I love startups. The chance to build, to create, to innovate. I was drawn in to the culture of entrepreneurship from the first moment I experienced it. However, I had all but written it off as a feasible career option after graduation for several reasons:

The risk associated with starting a business after college with very few resources was daunting.

There was no direct link to join an existing startup through campus recruiting.

This route was somewhat stigmatized as a path reserved only for those crazy enough not to want a typical white-collar job.

Enter Venture for America, a program designed so that young, talented grads spend two years in the trenches of a startup. In effect, Venture for America brings the recruiting and resources startups lack to graduates like me who are looking for a way in.

I was sold. And as I read more about the program, I began to realize something astounding: my truest and deepest beliefs and values were central to the mission and goals of this program.

Finally, I no longer felt crazy. After using my energy and abilities in the wrong place for so long, I wanted to finally redirect them toward something I cared about. I wanted a fulfilling career that aligned with my beliefs and values. I wanted to see my actions have a real impact on the organization I worked for and create change for the common good. And most important, I wanted to stand for something that matters. This was my chance.

Appendix D: Job Traits

It took me several years in different companies to determine what job traits were important to me. When I was still in school, I started out with a very basic set of criteria:

1. Intellectual versus manual. Does the job require a lot of conceptual work where I use my brain?

2. Higher pay versus lower pay. Will I get paid a lot? I didn't have any real numbers in mind, but more money seemed better than less.

These criteria alone didn't prove to be very useful.

Later, I realized that there's one big question people should ask when choosing a job: Is this company on a growth path? If it is, life is likely to be a whole lot more interesting and rewarding. This conclusion stemmed from the other job traits I discovered made a job more enjoyable:

3. Changing over time versus repetition. In some environments, roles shift and change each period, depending on what the company's needs are. You do something a little bit different each day, week, or month because the company itself is changing. In other environments, many functional roles can become very repetitive if you perform similar tasks over and over again.

4. Broad development versus specialization and efficiency. Some jobs want you to become excellent at something highly particular (e.g., cutting people's knees open and fixing them). On the other end of the spectrum is a role through which you're required to develop new skills because of evolving responsibilities (e.g., a manager at a growing company). Think a scalpel (specialist) versus a Swiss Army knife (generalist). Many young people get attracted to acquiring a specialized skill or expertise because it seems marketable. But the potential downside of certain roles is that you will utilize one skill to the exclusion of others.

5. Managing and teaching others versus operating individually. Some positions involve developing others and taking responsibility for larger groups of people (e.g., the head of a sales department). On the other hand, many of those with specialized skills or creative roles operate independently much of the time (e.g., a lawyer, doctor, accountant, designer/artist, writer, and the like). It's good to ask yourself, do you like being alone with a complex task for an extended period of time, or do you prefer working with others in a team setting? In most professional settings you're largely solo; one might say that lawyers and doctors work together, but often they have their heads down, drafting a document or examining a patient.

6. Autonomy and agency versus low discretion. In some jobs, you are able to make choices on how best to address a particular problem, and can exert some control over your own environment and schedule. In other roles, your discretion can be quite limited due to detailed hierarchies, policies, and procedures. For example, I found that I had relatively limited discretion as a lawyer at a big firm because my schedule and environment were out of my control, the client made most of the big decisions, and there was generally a "correct" way to do things. You're also likely to feel more empowered if the organization is more collegial and less hierarchical.

7. People- and service-oriented organizations versus institutions. In some organizations (e.g., a tutoring business, a restaurant or bar, a personal financial advisory firm, a medical practice), you directly serve people whom you may even see face-to-face. In others, as is common in many professional service contexts, your clients are large organizations that are hard to personalize (e.g., consulting for a large pharmaceutical company, helping a cable company buy a media property, and so on). Many people find it more engaging or invigorating to be able to personally identify with the beneficiaries of the work you're doing. It's one reason why, for example, working in a restaurant or as a camp counselor is kind of enjoyable—you make people happy for a while and walk out with a little stack of small bills.

8. Compensation for value versus compensation for time. In most established organizations, there are firm compensation and advancement guidelines, and they're generally related to how long you've been there. As a lawyer, consultant, or accountant you bill by the hour based on seniority. As a doctor or dentist you likely bill per patient treated or procedure administered.

As another example, when my father generated a patent,

IBM paid him a bonus of a few hundred dollars regardless of the actual value of the patent. Even if he were to create significant value for the company, it would not be reflected in compensation. This is sort of appropriate because of the security—my dad wanted to be able to go to the lab each day and not be under the gun to produce some breakthrough to feed his family. (Plus, his lab equipment was expensive.)

In a startup or growth company context, it's possible for an individual to be compensated according to the value she adds. In particular, if you're an early team member you can be rewarded for a company's success with increased responsibilities and compensation in addition to potential equity. If your team succeeds, you benefit—sometimes quite dramatically. If your team doesn't succeed, then not much value was created, and you probably won't get paid all that much.

9. Creative process versus established process. If a company has done something before, it probably has a set of documentation, rules, and policies to apply, and as an employee you will be expected to follow the process. There is a "correct" way to do things, and deviations aren't typically considered a positive thing. Accounting would be an example: there's a well-defined process that should lead to a certain result.

In other settings, either because of the nature of the activity or because it hasn't been done before, you may innovate or implement something new. There is less of a road map when organizations are trying to get market adoption or develop a new offering. Since these processes are intrinsically somewhat less prescribed, you'll likely be figuring things out with a fresh eye (though if you're smart you'll often refer to other companies' best practices). For me, breaking new ground and attempting to spur growth is often a whole lot more enjoyable than patrolling territory that was claimed long ago.

10. Building or making progress versus maintaining position. If a company is growing, then people's roles often change and opportunities abound. You are much more likely to feel that you are building toward something and making progress with each passing month. Every day you put a brick in place, and eventually you look up and you've built a wall. It's very gratifying. Plus, growth covers up a lot of mistakes.

If a company is fighting a defensive battle, contracting, or even staying level, opportunities are harder to come by and roles tend to be more stagnant. There's more internal pressure for people to protect themselves because the pie isn't growing. Opportunities are harder to come by.

In a professional service environment, each deal or client engagement is generally starting from scratch. You work on one engagement or deal after another, with one ending as the next begins. Yes, you build experience and perhaps a tool kit for the next engagement, but it's a new deal every period (or worse, no new deal; idleness is a terrible state for a service provider).

11. Executing versus analyzing. In many analytical roles you synthesize a great deal of data to produce a report, build a projection, or make a recommendation. The output is the report, projection, or recommendation (e.g., as a consultant you build a report streamlining a company's sourcing). In an executive capacity, your output is the action or activity of the organization (e.g., opening stores, choosing what goods to sell, allocating resources to different marketing campaigns). It can be better to be the person taking recommendations and deciding what to do than the person figuring out what to recommend.

12. Team orientation versus individual metrics. In many professional service environments, the unit of performance is based on the individual (e.g., how many hours lawyers have worked, or how many patients doctors have seen or operated on). Each person can see how much the other partners brought in or billed. In most company contexts, the organization's performance is measured more collectively because people from different departments are required to work together in order to achieve shared goals. This can, in the best of worlds, lead to a more team-oriented culture and environment.

13. The uncertain path versus the predictable track. In some situations, you can say with some certainty what the path forward is going to look like over the next number of years in terms of career progression. At a large established firm, perhaps you're considered for a promotion every one to two years, with associate, manager, and director roles clearly laid out. In a more fluid growth environment, your path forward will vary widely depending on how the company does and your role within it. For example, you could be a manager at a company that is just raising its first investment round and is not sure what the next several years are going to look like.

14. Sense of ownership versus being an employee. In some companies, staff members feel a sense of ownership over their work and the performance of the company due to the nature of the activity, company age and size, culture, or compensation mechanisms (e.g., stock ownership). At a small or new company, you can legitimately feel that your activities are going to influence the success or failure of the enterprise each day. Some large companies have taken great pains to maintain a sense of ownership among staff members even as the company has grown (e.g., Southwest Airlines is known for a great business culture and managed to avoid layoffs even in the teeth of the recession). In other environments, employees feel detached from their employer and see individual performance and company performance as largely unrelated. In these companies, individuals are often much more concerned with their own individual progression than pushing the organization forward.

15. Being well regarded versus obscurity and negativity. Certain roles and organizations are admired by employees' families, peers, friends, and the community at large. Others are not as well regarded or well known.

This is a pretty big motivator for young people in particular. One of the first questions you get asked in social contexts is, "What do you do?"

If you say that you work at a startup, often people will press and try and see if the company is "legit." They'll ask what it does, how it's funded, who's behind it, and other such questions. It's an irritating facet of entrepreneurship that you defy ready classification in social settings. If the company eventually does well the conversation gets easy.*

16. Long-term versus transactional relationships. In some industries and roles it is customary for employees to come and go every couple of years—particularly junior hires.

---

*For what it's worth, many of my friends had very little idea what I did for a living throughout my twenties, and would introduce me as a lawyer for years after I'd left the law firm.

In other environments employees may be expected to stay for extended periods of time and build long-term relationships.

17. Positive impact versus neutral or indeterminate impact. Some organizations have missions or conduct activities that produce a discernible, positive impact (e.g., developing a new technology that reduces pollution or improves a health care treatment). Other companies conduct activities that are neutral or unclear in impact.

SUMMARY LIST:
1. Intellectual versus manual
2. Higher pay versus lower pay
3. Changing over time versus repetition
4. Broad development versus specialization and efficiency
5. Managing and teaching others versus operating individually
6. Autonomy and responsibility versus low discretion
7. People- and service-oriented organizations versus institutions
8. Compensation for value versus compensation for time
9. Creative process versus established process
10. Building or making progress versus maintaining position
11. Executing versus analyzing
12. Team orientation versus individual metrics
13. The uncertain path versus the predictable track
14. Sense of ownership versus being an employee
15. Being well regarded versus obscurity and negativity
16. Long-term versus transactional relationships
17. Positive impact versus neutral or indeterminate impact

I've found this more detailed framework much more useful than my original "highly paid thought work" construction, and I hope others find it helpful as well. Each person will respond to and weigh each factor differently. But the goal should be to figure out which of these you care about and find a role that fits.

It's unrealistic to expect a job to hit every single or a majority of notes, particularly when starting out. Every job has its fair share of trade-offs and a need to manage relationships. For example, the founder of a business will, years into it, be doing a fair amount of repetitive stuff. That's the nature of work. But this set of job traits may help identify why particular roles are more or less appealing to you, and it's useful to have a vision of what kind of role you'd like to move toward.

This is also indicative of what kind of organization you'd want to work for. Being the 5001st employee at a company is a very different experience from being the 15th. Some companies have it all figured out, and some haven't. On one extreme is being CEO of your own company or working for a small company just starting out, where you care about your colleagues and want to see everyone succeed. On the other end is working for a big firm with established processes for another big client that you may not have much of an emotional stake in.

If you're wired like me, you'll look for a small, early-stage growth company that's led by people you respect and feel you could learn from. It should be addressing a genuine need and operating responsibly. The company doesn't need to be saving the planet or doing something you're innately passionate about, though that would be great. If it's the right kind of organization, the role will in all likelihood be one that is thinking, broad, changing, managing, deciding, rewarding, creating, progressing, doing, collaborative, risk taking, committed, owning, and contributing. There's a chance it may not work out. But whether your job becomes compensated or admired will be at least a little bit up to you.

Appendix E: 2012 Venture Fellows and Their Employers

Everyone who becomes part of Venture for America will always owe a debt to this first class.

DETROIT

Brentt Baltimore: Investment banker at Credit Suisse from Los Angeles who turned down an offer from a hedge fund to join Venture for America; cofounder of the Startup Effect. (Detroit Venture Partners)

Brian Bosche: Dartmouth grad and founder of a basketball league who grew up in Montana and California; cofounder of the Startup Effect. (Bizdom U).

Gabby Bryant: Economics major from Harvard who wanted to go back to her hometown of Detroit and do her part to rebuild the city. (Dandelion Detroit, Detroit Institute of the Arts)

Kathy Cheng: MIT economics and urban planning major from New Jersey who had worked at the US Small Business Administration; working on a food truck. (Doodle Home)

Tim Dingman: Electrical engineer from Brown who ran a design conference and founded Eco-Flow, a company specializing in showerhead efficiency upgrades for college dorms; cofounder of Rebirth Realty in Detroit. (Accio Energy)

Jake L'Ecuyer: Michigan native and Michigan State grad who had worked for several startups while still a student. (Benzinga)

Scott Lowe: Engineering physics major from the University of Oklahoma who built an online portal and cofounded Rebirth Realty to rehab a foreclosed Detroit house for Venture Fellows. (Digerati, Chalkfly)

Todd Nelson: Columbia grad in environmental science and history from North Carolina with a strong bent toward renewable energy. (NextEnergy)

Max Nussenbaum: Ultra-creative Wesleyan grad who had written a play and had competed on *Who Wants to be a Millionaire?*; cofounder of Rebirth Realty. (Are You a Human)

Brian Rudolph: New York native who started multiple businesses while at Emory, working on a high-protein pasta business. (Quikly)

Derek Turner: Columbia anthropology major from Phoenix who had written about heading to Detroit before Venture for America, and brought his fiancée Katie to Detroit; Katie then started working at another startup. (Ambassador, Grand Circus)

Charles Watkins: Yale grad from Detroit who wanted to return home and rebuild the city. (Rock Ventures, Google)

NEW ORLEANS

Mark Bernstein: Northwestern University economics and environmental science, engineering, and policy major from Chicago. (Resource Environmental Solutions)

Sara Cullen: Gregarious Cornell grad from Oregon who was the first in her family to attend college. (Carrollton Group, RPM and Company)

Edie Feinstein: Industrial and labor relations major from Cornell who ran a foodie club on campus and started a food blog. (Kickboard)

Mike Mayer: Wharton finance major from Florida who turned down an investment bank to head to New Orleans; cofounder of Startup Effect. (Federated Sample)

John McGrail: Fulbright Scholar and economics and Russian major from Amherst College who had been captain of the cross-country team. (TurboSquid)

Billy Schrero: Tulane grad from Chicago who had been a Social Innovation Fellow at the Center for Engaged Learning and Teaching in New Orleans; cofounder of Startup Effect. (StaffInsight)

Alison Schmitt: Wharton School economics major from New Jersey oriented toward economic development and education. (EMH Strategy)

Nihal Shrinath: Computer science major from Amherst College who had also been editor of the school's newspaper. (VoiceHIT, Resource Environmental Solutions)

Sam Stites: Math and physics major and computer programmer from Vassar; circus performer. (TurboSquid)

PROVIDENCE

Ethan Carlson: Yale mechanical engineer from Minnesota dedicated to clean energy. (VCharge)

Melanie Friedrichs: Brown economics major and ultimate

Frisbee co-captain, organized social entrepreneurship conference in Rhode Island. (Andera)

Sean Lane: Boston College communications major who co-founded a hockey clinic and served as codirector for his college sports radio station. (Swipely)

Sean Pennino: Physics and entrepreneurship major from Notre Dame and Brown; originally from Rochester, New York. (Teespring)

Bryant Yik: Finance major from the Wharton School who took apart computers as a youngster. (MoFuse, Teespring)

LAS VEGAS

All Venture Fellows work in association with Downtown Project, Tony Hsieh's $350 million initiative to revitalize downtown Las Vegas.

Ovik Banerjee: Environmental science and biology major at University of North Carolina who had led a fellowship program in college. (Downtown Project)

Laura Berk: Economics major at Williams College; from Virginia. (Vegas Tech Project)

Andy Chatham: From Rhode Island; head of Cornell Student Agencies and founded and led Cornell entrepreneurship organization. (Project 100)

Barry Conrad: Business major from Colorado who'd worked at a venture capital firm and won a business plan competition while at the University of Oklahoma. (Small Business team)

Josh Levine: Wesleyan grad and New Haven, Connecticut, native interested in health care and urban development. (Turntable Health)

Rob Solomon: Cornell presidential scholar from upstate New York who had rowed varsity crew and cofounded a music blog. (Small Business team)

Austin Jude Stanion: North Carolina native; creative head of an improv comedy troupe at University of North Carolina. (Project 100)

CINCINNATI

Dan Bloom: Wrestling champion and history major from Wesleyan, working on a sandwich shop. (Blackbook HR)

Max Eisenberg: Washington University in St. Louis urban studies and entrepreneurship grad who had bought and run a business in college. (Ilesfay)

James Fayal: Finance major from the University of Maryland who had interned at Morgan Stanley (CincyTech, NextFab Studio)

Rickey Ishida: Cornell biomedical engineer who rebuilt his own house. (Zipscene, MakerGear)

Jim Kahmann: Columbia varsity crew athlete and economics major, working on Action Hero Boot Camp. (OneMorePallet)

Chelsea Koglmeier: President of the Duke triathlon team and a Cincinnati native. (The Brandery, Roadtrippers)

Roanne Lee: Georgetown grad from Los Angeles who had interned at a venture capital boutique and 20th Century Fox. (Cintrifuse)

Appendix F: The Postgraduate Paths of National University Graduates

U nfortunately, the data on what national university graduates do is found in different formats in different places. One can get a pretty good picture of what national university graduates do from publicly available information, but in many cases some estimating and ballparking are necessary.

The *New York Times* published a breakdown of Harvard, Yale, and Princeton postgraduation employment as reported by the career services offices of each of these schools.[1] Harvard also publishes post-graduate info on its website.[2] Between 17 and 28 percent of employed Harvard seniors went into financial services between 2008 and 2011, with 12 to 19 percent of employed seniors going into management consulting during the same period. Career services estimates that 61 percent of Harvard seniors were employed after graduation in 2011, so we can find an absolute range.[3]

Harvard, like most colleges, lumps law school together with graduate programs (e.g., PhDs in economics) into "full-time graduate or professional school." However, the Law

School Admissions Council (LSAC) helpfully publishes data on the number of people applying to law school each year from the top 240 "feeder schools."[4] For 2011, the last available year, the number of applicants to law school ranged from 214 (11 percent) at Columbia to 316 (24 percent) at Yale, with Harvard weighing in at 320 (19 percent). These numbers are higher than those resulting from senior surveys because graduates often work for a year or two in unrelated fields (e.g., nonprofit organizations, in education, and so on) before applying to law school. The LSAC numbers are much more telling because they show how many graduates apply to law school from each college every year, sometimes several years after graduation.

One has to estimate a little bit to go from the applicant numbers to matriculants. In 2011, 82 percent of admitted applicants went on to attend law school.[5] If we assume that applicants from elite schools are 80 percent likely to get into at least one program and attend at the normal rate, then we would discount the applicant numbers from each school by about 35 percent to find matriculants. We thus estimate that between 65 and 90 percent of law school applicants from national universities matriculate. The range has historically been several percentage points higher than the 2011 numbers and is likely to decline further—people don't regard law school as a universally wise investment anymore.

The Association of American Medical Colleges similarly reports the number of applicants from undergraduate institutions each year.[6] In 2012, the range of med school applicants among top schools was approximately 16 percent, ranging from 10 percent at Columbia (201 applicants) to 22 percent at Duke (360 applicants), with 307 Harvard grads (about 17 percent of the 1,665 seniors) being representative. These are also inflated relative to the number of matriculants—the number of applicants in 2011 was 43,919, with 19,230 students enrolled, for a matriculation rate of 44 percent. However, from the top schools the admissions rate is likely to be much higher: we estimate that the vast majority of students who finished the pre-med requirements at a national university (many aspiring doctors are weeded out by the difficult science curriculum at these schools during their freshman or sophomore years) who also went on to take the MCAT and apply would go on to attend medical school. Our range is thus 65 to 90 percent med school applicants from these universities would go on to matriculate.

Harvard's statistics show 17 percent of graduates heading to law school or graduate school. If we project that roughly half of the Harvard graduates who go to law school go directly from college (historically the case), approximately 8 to 9 percent head to master's or PhD programs in various disciplines. We can make a similar estimate at other schools where applicable.

Teach for America reports the universities from which it recruits the most corps members each year. In 2012, Northwestern (63), Harvard (62), Georgetown (61), Cornell (59), University of Pennsylvania (41), Dartmouth (37), Washington University in St. Louis (36), Brown (36), Yale (35), Duke (34), Columbia (32), Princeton (27) and the University of Chicago (27) each sent dozens of new teachers to Teach for America, which recruited 5,800 recent graduates in 2012.[7] These numbers were relatively constant from 2011, which saw similar concentrations from Harvard (66), Duke (53), Penn (53),

Brown (49), Cornell (49), Northwestern (49), Yale (41), Stanford (30), Columbia (36), and Johns Hopkins (25), University of Chicago (24), Princeton (23) and Dartmouth (20) for TFA's 2011 corps of 5,200.[8] Teach for America has become the sixth most popular path for national university graduates after finance, consulting, law, medicine, and grad school. Its operating budget in 2011 was $219 million, of which $37.6 million went to recruitment and selection of new teachers.

According to Princeton's Career Services office, as cited in Rampell's *New York Times* article, between 33.4 and 46 percent of employed seniors from Princeton went on to work in financial services between 2000 and 2010. Princeton career services also published a report that 64.3 percent had accepted employment in 2012 and 61.6 percent in 2011.[9] The "services" category, which includes consulting, had a range of 25.6 to 37 percent of employed Princeton seniors from 2000 to 2010. We assume that consulting comprises the vast majority of the "services" category for our estimate. For graduate school, Princeton estimates that 22.8 percent went straight to graduate or professional school in 2012. We project that roughly 14 to 16 percent are those going straight to law school or med school, which would leave 7 to 9 percent going to graduate school, consistent with Princeton's peer institutions.

Yale's numbers, as reported in the *New York Times* article, indicate that between 14 percent and 31 percent of employed seniors went to business/financial services from 2000 to 2010. In 2010, 75 percent of the class had jobs a year after graduation, so one can pretty easily see what percent of the class went into finance that year (10.5 percent in 2010, roughly 19.5 percent for the class of 2008).[10] "Industry" here includes management consulting, so consulting itself is difficult to break out—hence, we take a very broad range for Yale's management consulting statistics. The *New York Times* article shows that 7 percent of Yale grads heading to arts and sciences (nonprofessional) graduate school in 2010.

The University of Pennsylvania reports its statistics for undergraduates each year.[11] In 2012, 31 percent of employed seniors went into finance and 20 percent went to consulting. Sixty-four percent were reported as employed, so again one can easily determine the total proportion.

As one would expect, the statistics from Wharton, Penn's elite undergraduate business school, are even more dramatic.[12] Over half of the Wharton Class of 2012 (251 out of 482) went to New York. The top employers were Goldman Sachs (32), Boston Consulting Group (17), Crédit Suisse (17), Morgan Stanley (17), Barclays Capital (16), McKinsey (14), BlackRock (12), Citi (12), JPMorgan Chase (11) and Bain and Company (10).

Cornell career services reports universitywide data.[13] In 2011, of those who were employed, 24.5 percent were in financial services and 14.2 percent were in consulting. Fifty percent of the class reported being employed. Fully 39.6 percent of employed respondents worked in New York City. Those going to graduate school made up 28.8 percent, with 28 percent of this subset attending law school or med school.

Duke University Career Services states that 15.5 percent of the class of 2012 went into financial services and 13.7 percent went into consulting, similar to 16.3 percent and 12.1 percent respectively in 2011.[14] The top five job locations in 2012 were New York (24 percent); North Carolina (15 percent); Washington, DC (11 percent); California (10 percent);

and Virginia (suburbs of DC) (8 percent). In 2011, the top five locations were New York; Washington, DC; Raleigh-Durham; San Francisco, and Boston. In 2012, 21 percent of graduates indicated they were pursuing further education, which included medical school, law school, and graduate school.

MIT has survey data from 2011 and 2012 available.[15] Top US locations for graduates in 2012 were Massachusetts (196), California (120), and New York (81). In 2011 the locations were Massachusetts (181), New York (95), and California (92). Financial services and investment banking (46) and consulting (47) were the top two sectors listed among 274 seniors who cited employers in 2012; these represented 17 percent for each. If we take the survey respondents as representative and use the 53 percent employment rate, the estimate is 9 percent for each in 2012. This was essentially the same as in 2011 (10 percent and 9.5 percent) and 2009 (8.8 percent and 9.4 percent for finance and consulting); 40 percent went on to graduate school, including medical school.[16]

Brown's Career Lab published survey data for 2012 that shows 15 percent of employed seniors (127) going into finance and banking and 9 percent (77) into consulting, with 13 percent to non-professional graduate schools.[17] This data was consistent with the statistics in 2011.

Information provided by Columbia University indicates that 56.8 percent of Columbia College and Engineering School graduates in 2012 were employed, with 19.6 percent heading into financial services and 9.7 percent into consulting. In 2011 the employment number was 55.7 percent, with 26.9 percent and 10.5 percent heading into financial services and consulting, respectively; 23 percent went on to graduate school in each year.[18]

Dartmouth's published statistics indicate that in 2008, 58 percent of its graduates were employed, with 33 percent indicating finance and 21 percent consulting (19 percent and 12 percent overall).[19] In 2009, 11.8 percent of employed seniors indicated consulting and 11.4 percent indicated financial services; the proportion of graduates that were employed overall was not indicated. In 2010, 56.2 percent were employed full-time, with 10.6 percent in financial services and 11 percent in consulting. In 2011, 64 percent were employed full-time, with 12.2 percent in financial services and 15 percent in consulting. During this period 18 to 21 percent of Dartmouth graduates indicated that they were attending or planning to attend graduate or professional school.

Although Stanford does not publish its statistics, an article in the *Stanford Daily* indicated that in 2010, over 15 percent of Stanford graduates went into financial services, the highest for any industry except consulting.[20] Law school, medical school, and Teach for America statistics are all available from other sources.

Johns Hopkins University posted data showing that 29 percent of graduates in 2010 and 2011 went on to business services, banking, consulting, and financial services; 41 percent were employed full-time, for a total of 12 percent heading into banking and consulting.[21] We can divide the 12 percent evenly into financial services and consulting. Thirty-seven percent went on to graduate or professional school, with the majority choosing fields other than medicine or law.

From the University of Chicago in 2011, 43 percent had accepted full-time employment offers, with 17 percent in banking/brokerage/finance and 16 percent in consulting. In 2012, the numbers were 21 percent to finance/general business and 10 percent to consulting, with 51 percent employed upon graduation and 71 percent within ten months of graduation.[22] In 2011, 19 percent were attending graduate programs, of which 74 percent were neither law school nor medical school programs. In 2012, 17 percent attended graduate school.

Georgetown publishes very detailed senior surveys each year.[23] Georgetown's 2012 stats show 16 percent of responding seniors heading into financial services and 13 percent to management consulting, about in line with their normal ranges over the previous several years.

My research assistant commented, "It's strange how these schools all gather and report data differently. This is important information—you'd think it would be all together somewhere." It's clear what the general picture is, but having more precise data that applied to different time periods (e.g., "How many people who get graduate degrees go on to work in which industry?") would be very illuminating.

Where our talent goes drives our economy—if we know where our smart people are going, we can tell the future.

Notes

Introduction

1. Ben Casselman, "Risk-Averse Culture Infects U.S. Workers, Entrepreneurs," *Wall Street Journal*, June 2, 2013, retrieved from http://online.wsj.com/article/SB10001424127887324031404578481162903760052.html.
2. Tim Kane, *The Importance of Startups in Job Creation and Job Destruction*, Kauffman Foundation Research Series: Firm Formation and Economic Growth (Kansas City, MO: Kauffman Foundation, 2010).
3. Zoltan J. Acs, William Parsons, and Spencer Tracy, *High-Impact Firms: Gazelles Revisited* (Washington, DC: Office of Advocacy, United States Small Business Administration, June 2008).

Chapter 1. The Prestige Pathways

1. A Harvard senior class survey in 2011 indicated that 16.5% of Harvard grads with jobs were working in financial services and 12.4% were in management consulting. See Harvard University Office of Career Services, Next Steps for Harvard Seniors: 2011," retrieved from http://www.ocs.fas.harvard.edu/students/jobs/seniorsurvey.htm. Law School Admissions Council statistics indicate that 320 Harvard grads applied to law school that year or approximately 20% of the graduating class of 1,650; see Law School Admissions Council, "Top 240 ABA Applicant Feeder Schools for Fall Applicants," retrieved from http://www.lsac.org/lsacresources/data/pdfs/top-240-feeder-schools.pdf. These statistics indicate those who are applying to law school in a given year (i.e., some of the 320 applicants in 2011 likely graduated in an earlier year and some 2011 graduates would apply later). The five-year average between 2006 and 2011 is 386 Harvard grads, or about 23% of each graduating class, applying to law school. The Harvard med school applicants for 2012 came to 17%. For med school

applicants by university, see Association of American Medical Colleges, "Table 2: Undergraduate Institutions Supplying Applicants to US Medical Schools by Applicant Race and Ethnicity, 2012," https://www.aamc.org/data/facts/applicantmatriculant/86042/table2.html; for more information, see appendix F.

2. Harvard University Office of Career Services, "Harvard College Seniors 2012: Next Steps," retrieved from http://www.ocs.fas.harvard.edu/next_steps.htm.

3. Ezra Klein, "Harvard's Liberal-Arts Failure Is Wall Street's Gain," retrieved from http://www.bloomberg.com/news/2012-02-16/harvard-liberal-arts-failure-is-wall-street-gain-commentary-by-ezra-klein.html.

4. Kevin Jack and James Brown,*Understanding the Financial Sector Meltdown: The Credit Crisis and NY's Financial Services Sector*. Albany, New York: New York State Department of Labor, Division of Research and Statistics.

5. John Horn and David Pleasance, "Restarting the US Small-Business Growth Engine," retrieved from http://www.mckinseyquarterly.com/Strategy/Growth/Restarting_the_US_small_business_growth_engine_3032.

Chapter 2. Too Much of a Good Thing

1. Andrew Lohse, "Lohse: A Corporate Stranglehold," *The Dartmouth*, August 2, 2011, retrieved from http://thedartmouth.com/2011/08/02/opinion/Corporate.

2. Richard Pérez-Peña, "Finance Jobs Still Appeal to Graduates at Dartmouth," retrieved from http://www.nytimes.com/2012/06/15/us/wall-street-appeal-remains-high-with-top-graduates.html.

3. See appendix F for detailed sources for this data for each listed university.

4. John Horn and David Pleasance, "Restarting the US Small-Business Growth Engine," retrieved from http://www.mckinseyquarterly.com/ Strategy/Growth/Restarting_the_US_small_business_growth_engine_3032.

5. See, for example, David A. Weinfeld, "Boycott Wall Street," *Harvard Crimson*, October 11, 2011, retrieved from http://www.thecrimson.com/article/2011/10/11/occupy-wall-street-harvard/; and Marina Keegan, "Even Artichokes Have Doubts," *Yale Daily News*, http://yaledailynews.com/weekend/2011/09/30/even-artichokes-have-doubts/.

6. Teryn Norris and Eli Pollak,. "Op-ed: Stop the Wall Street Recruitment," *Stanford Daily*, October 11, 2011, retrieved from http://www.stanforddaily.com/2011/10/11/op-ed-stop-the-wall-street-recruitment/.

7. James Kwak, "Why Do Harvard Kids Head to Wall Street?" *Baseline Scenario*, May 4, 2010, retrieved from http://baselinescenario.com/2010/05/04/why-do-harvard-kids-head-to-wall-street/.

8. Ezra Klein, "Why Do Harvard Kids Head to Wall Street? An Inter-

view with an ex-Wall Street Recruit." *Washington Post*, April 23, 2010, retrieved from http://voices.washingtonpost.com/ezra-klein/2010/04/why_do_harvard_kids_head_to_wa.html.

9. Ben Branham and Barbara Pruitt "The Cannibalization of Entrepreneurship in America: Expanding Financial Sector Depleting Pool of Potential High-Growth Company Founders," March 25, 2011, retrieved from http://www.kauffman.org/newsroom/expanding-financial-sector-depleting-pool-of-potential-high-growth-company-founders.aspx.

10. Anthony Ha, "Sequoia's Bryan Schreier Says It's Time for the Ivy Leagues to Embrace Startups," February 25, 2013, retrieved from http://techcrunch.com/2013/02/15/east-coast-vs-west-coast/.

Chapter 3. Professional Training Cuts Both Ways

1. A friend told me his firm's internal number over dinner. Consultancy staff attrition rates are often over 20% industrywide. Top-Consultant.com's Management Consultancy, *Recruitment Channel Report 2012*, retrieved from http://www.top-consultant.com/top-consultant_2012_recruitment_channel_report.pdf.

Chapter 4. Network Effects and Why Human Capital Markets Don't Self-Correct

1. "What Next for the Start-up Nation?" *Economist*, January 21, 2012, retrieved from http://www.economist.com/node/21543151.

2. Leon Lazaroff, "China to Capitalize on Nasdaq Jump with Tech IPOs, BNY Says," retrieved from http://www.bloomberg.com/news/2012-05-07/china-to-take-advantage-of-nasdaq-jump-with-tech-ipos-bny-says.html.

3. "Israel GDP Annual Growth Rate," retrieved from http://www.trading economics.com/israel/gdp-growth-annual.

4. Mark Gerson, quoted in Dan Senor and Saul Singer, *Start-up Nation: The Story of Israel's Economic Miracle* (New York: Twelve, 2009), 74–75.

5. Laurent Haug, quoted in Senor and Singer, *Start-up Nation*, 88.

6. See "Highest 4-Year Graduation Rates," *US News and World Report*, retrieved from http://colleges.usnews.rankingsandreviews.com/best-colleges/rankings/highest-grad-rate. Note that a high graduation rate within four years is a feature primarily of elite US colleges; the national six-year graduation rate for students starting a bachelor's program is only 58%, even accounting for the extra two years. See National Center for Education Statistics, "Fast Facts: Graduation Rates," retrieved from http://nces.ed.gov/fastfacts/display.asp?id=40.

7. Top universities are receiving more and more applicants, and their acceptance rates are thus at record lows. See Kayla Webley, "College Admissions: Iy League Acceptance Rates Decline," *Time*, April 2, 2013, retrieved from http://nation.time.com/2013/04/02/ivy-league-schools-accepting-even-fewer-kids/.

8. William Fitzsimmons, Marilyn E. McGrath, and Charles Ducey, "Time Out or Burn Out for the Next Generation," retrieved from http://www.admissions.college.harvard.edu/apply/time_off/index.html.

9. See, for example Elizabeth F. Brown, "Is Law School a Good Investment?" letter to the editor, *New York Times*, December 4, 2012, retrieved from http://www.nytimes.com/opinion/ /is-law-school-a-good-investment.html; and Joe Queenan, "Law Schools and Other Shameless Schemes," *Wal Street Journal*, March 15, 2007, retrieved from http://online.wsj.com/article/SB10001424127887323339330457835 8583587338070.html.

10. Ethan Bronner, "Law Schools' Applications Fall as Costs Rise and Jobs Are Cut," *New York Times*, January 31, 2013, retrieved from http://www.nytimes.com/education/law-schools-applications-fall-as-costs-rise-and-jobs-are-cut.html?pagewanted=all.

11. American Bar Association, "Enrollment and Degrees Awarded 1963—2012 Academic Years," retrieved from http://www.americanbar.org/content/dam/aba/administrative/legal_education_and_admissions_to_the_bar/statistics/enrollment_degrees_awarded.authcheckdam.pdf.

12. "Class of 2011 Has Lowest Employment Rate Since Class of 1994," retrieved from http://www.nalp.org/0712research. At least one analysis has suggested that as many as 90% of law school graduates will not have legal jobs waiting for them upon graduation; see Graham Martin, "Lawyer Jobs Account for Only 10% of New Law School Grads per Year," retrieved from http://lawyerist.com/lawyer-jobs-employ-ten-percent-new-grads/.

13. Paul M. Barrett, "Howrey's Bankruptcy and Big Law Firms' Small Future," *Bloomberg Businessweek*, May 2, 2013, retrieved from http://www.businessweek.com/articles/2013-05-02/howreys-bankruptcy-and-big-law-firms-small-future.

14. Debra Cassens Weiss, "Law Schools Could Be Admitting 80 Percent of Their Applicants This Fall, Statistics Suggest." *ABA Journal*, August 9, 2012, retrieved from http://www.abajournal.com/news/article/law_schools_could_be_admitting_80_percent_of_their_applicants_this_fall_sta.

15. The twenty-two-year old could rely on employment statistics, but these have been shown to be inflated by some institutions to include jobs that don't require the degree in question. See, for example, Karen Sloan, "ABA Seeks Help Monitoring Law Graduate Employment Statistics," *National Law* Journal, February 21, 2013, retrieved from http://www.law.com/jsp/nlj/PubArticleNLJ.jsp?id=1202589105681&ABA_seeks_help_monitoring_law_graduate_employment_statistics_&slreturn=201303231016

15. A study by McKinsey and Company showed that half of graduates didn't look at graduation rates when picking a college, and four in ten didn't look at job-placement or salary records. See McKinsey and Company, *Voice of the Graduate*, retrieved from http://mckinseyonso

ciety.com/downloads/reports/Education/UXC001%20Voice%20of%20
the%20Graduate%20v7.pdf.

Chapter 5. Building Things Is Really Hard

1. "Industry Survey: How Much Does It Cost to Open a Restaurant?"
retrieved from http://www.restaurantowner.com/public/811.cfm.
2. Max Nisen, "The 'Devil's Triangle' Keeps Most Startups from
Growing into Full-Fledged Businesses," retrieved from http://www
.businessinsider.com/how-to-get-past-the-devils-triangle-that-kills-
company-growth-2013-2.
3. Alyson Shontell, "The Story of a Failed Startup and a Founder Driven
to Suicide," retrieved from http://www.businessinsider.com/jody-
sherman-ecomom-2013-4. Dave's still alive and well; the article's
about someone else.
4. Paul Allen, "My Favorite Mistake," retrieved from http://www.thedai
lybeast.com/newsweek/2011/04/24/my-favorite-mistake.html.
5. Mark Cuban, "Ten Questions for Mark Cuban" interview, *Forbes*, November 4, 2010, retrieved from http://www.forbes.com/2010/11/03/
billionare-mark-cuban-entrepreneur-dallas-mavericks-secrets-self-
made-10.html.

Chapter 7. Running a Company

1. Only about 1% of businesses ever receive venture capital. See Ros-
sana Weitekampand Barbara Pruitt, "US Venture Capital Industry Must Shrink to Be an Economic Force, Kauffman Foundation
Study Finds," press release, retrieved from http://bx.businessweek
.com/venture-capital/view?url=http%3A%2F%2F;www.kauffman.org
%2Fnewsroom%2Fventure-capital-industry-must-shrink-to-be-an-ec
onomic-force-kauffman-foundation-study-finds.aspx.

Chapter 8. Rent-Seeking versus Value Creation

1. Anita Raghavan, "High I.P.O. Fees Weigh on US Firms, Study Finds,"
New York Times, December 30, 2010, retrieved from http://dealbook.ny
times.com/2010/12/30/high-i-p-o-fees-weigh-on-u-s-firms-study-finds/.
2. Telis Demos, "Exactly What is a Dutch Auction?" *Wall Street Journal*,
June 21, 2012, retrieved from http://blogs.wsj.com/deals/2012/06/21/
exactly-what-is-a-dutch-auction/.
3. See "Underwriter Rankings: 8/9/2012–8/9/2013," retrieved from http://
www.renaissancecapital.com/IPOHome/Underwriter/urankings.aspx
?list=proceeds. Underwriter fees are typically about 6% of an IPO's
value.
4. See National Resident Matching Program, *Results and Data: 2012
Main Residency Match*, retrieved from http://www.nrmp.org/data/re
sultsanddata2012.pdf.
5. Some of this story appears as part of an interview with Walker on Forbes
.com. See Alexander Taub, "Teespring: Is This Rhode Island Based

Startup the Future of Custom Apparel?" *Forbes*, January 3, 2013, retrieved from http://www.forbes.com/sites/alextaub/2013/01/03/teespring-is-this-rhode-island-based-startup-the-future-of-custom-apparel/.

Chapter 9. The Qualitites We Need
1. See Reid Hoffman and Ben Casnocha, *The Start-up of You: Adapt to the Future, Invest in Yourself, and Transform Your Career* (New York: Random House, 2012).

Chapter 10. Building a Machine to Fix the Machine
1. For the current list of the Venture for America board members see http://www.ventureforamerica.org/team.
2. To get a more complete sense of these info sessions, a fifteen-minute recording of a talk I gave at Georgetown is available at http://ventureforamerica.org/andrew-yang-tedx-talk-fixing-the-flow-of-human-capital/
3. See Barbara E. Hernandez, "Mark Zuckerberg: 'I Should Have Stayed in Boston,'" November 1, 2011, retrieved from http://www.nbcsandiego.com/blogs/press-here/Mark-Zuckerberg-I-Should-Have-Stayed-in-Boston-132938528.html; and Jessica Guynn, "Zuckerberg: If I Started Facebook Today, I Would Stay in Boston," *Los Angeles Times*, October 31, 2011, retrieved from http://latimesblogs.latimes.com/technology/2011/10/mark-zuckerberg-facebook-boston.html.

Chapter 11. The Future Changes for at Least a Few
1. Amy S. Blackwood, Katie L. //Roeger, and Sarah L. Pettijohn, *The Nonprofit Sector in Brief: Public Charities, Giving, and Volunteering, 2012*, retrieved from http://www.urban.org/UploadedPDF/412674-The-Nonprofit-Sector-in-Brief.pdf.
2. Dan Pallotta, "Why Can't We Sell Charity Like We Sell Perfume?" *Wall Street Journal*, September 14, 2012, retrieved from http://online.wsj.com/article/SB10000872396390444017504577647502309260064.html.
3. Molly F. Sherlock and Jane G. Gravelle, *An Overview of the Nonprofit and Charitable Sector* (Washington, DC: Congressional Research Service, 2009). From 1970 to 2009, the proportion of charitable giving in the United States has hovered around 2%, peaking at 2.37% in 2005 before declining back to 2.1% in 2009.
4. Kristin Ivie, "Want to Start a Nonprofit? Think Again," September 29, 2009, retrieved from http://casefoundation.org/print/1190961.

Chapter 14. How to Get Smart People to Build Things
1. Enrico Moretti, "Where the Good Jobs Are—and Why: When a High-Tech Company Hires One Person, Five Other New Jobs Follow." *Wall Street Journal*, September 17, 2013. Retrieved from http://online.wsj.com/article/SB10001424127887324576304579072773954985630.html.

Appendix F: The Postgraduate Paths for National University Graduates

1. Catherine Rampell, "Out of Harvard, and into Finance," *New York Times*, December 21, 2011, retrieved from http://economix.blogs.nytimes.com/2011/12/21/out-of-harvard-and-into-finance/.
2. Harvard University Office of Career Services, "Harvard College Seniors 2012: Next Steps," retrieved from http://www.ocs.fas.harvard.edu/next_steps.htm. Each year, the Harvard student newspaper, the *Harvard Crimson*, publishes its own senior surveys, which present slightly different numbers. We decided to use the numbers provided by career services, but the *Crimson*'s surveys can easily be found online.
3. Harvard Office of Career Services, retrieved from http://www.ocs.fas.harvard.edu/students/jobs/seniorsurvey.htm.
4. Law School Admissions Council, "Top 240 ABA Applicant Feeder Schools for Fall Applicants," retrieved from http://www.lsac.org/lsacresources/data/pdfs/top-240-feeder-schools.pdf.
5. Law School Admissions Council, "Data: LSAC Volume Summary," retrieved from http://www.lsac.org/lsacresources/data/lsac-volume-summary.asp.
6. Association of American Medical Colleges, "Table 2: Undergraduate Institutions Supplying Applicants to US Medical Schools by Applicant Race and Ethnicity, 2012," retrieved from https://www.aamc.org/data/facts/applicantmatriculant/86042/table2.html.
7. "Top Colleges and Universities Contributing Graduating Seniors to TFA's 2012 Teaching Corps," retrieved from http://www.teachforamerica.org/sites/default/files/2012.Top_.Contributors.pdf.
8. See "Top Colleges and Universities Contributing to Teach For America's 2011 Teaching Corps," retrieved from http://www.teachforamerica.org/sites/default/files/Top%20Contributors%20List%202011_Color_0.pdf
9. See Princeton University Career Services, *Annual Report 2011–2012*, retrieved from http://issuu.com/pucareerservices/docs/princeton_career_services_2011-2012_annual?mode=window.
10. Yale University Office of Institutional Research's Factsheet Archive, retrieved at http://oir.yale.edu/factsheet-archive.
11. University of Pennsylvania Career Services, "Preliminary Career Plans Survey Report: Class of 2012," retrieved from http://www.vpul.upenn.edu/careerservices/files/Classof2012CareerPlans_preliminary_1354568029.pdf.
12. University of Pennsylvania Career Services Career Plan Survey Reports, "Wharton Undergraduate Class of 2012 Career Plans Survey Report," retrieved from http://www.vpul.upenn.edu/careerservices/files/WHA_2012cp.pdf.
13. Cornell University Career Services, "Preliminary Class of 2011 Postgraduate Report," retrieved from http://www.career.cornell

241

.edu/resources/surveys/upload/PreliminaryClassOf2011.pdf.

14. Duke University Student Affairs, "Career Center Senior Survey," retrieved from http://studentaffairs.duke.edu/career/statistics-reports#node-870

15. MIT Global Education and Career Development, *Graduating Student Survey: June 2011 Survey Results*, retrieved from http://gecd.mit.edu/sites/default/files/graduation11.pdf; and MIT Global Education and Career Development, *Graduating Student Survey: June 2012 Survey Results*, retrieved from http://gecd.mit.edu/sites/default/files/graduation12.pdf.

16. For another analysis of MIT employment, see "MIT Students after Graduation," retrieved from http://www.universityparent.com/2009/08/20/mit-students-after-graduation.

17. Brown University Career Lab, "Class of 2012 Immediate Postgraduate Plans," retrieved from http://brown.edu/campus-life/support/careerlab/postgrad-data/class-2012-immediate-postgraduate-plans.

18. Columbia University Center for Career Education, "2012 Graduating Student Survey Results," retrieved from http://www.careereducation.columbia.edu/students/data/2012.

19. Dartmouth University Office of Institutional Research, "Survey Research and Reports," retrieved from http://www.dartmouth.edu/~oir/surveyresearchreports.html.

20. Teryn Norris and Eli Pollak, "Op-ed: Stop the Wall Street Recruitment," *Stanford Daily*, October 11, 2011, retrieved from http://www.stanforddaily.com/2011/10/11/op-ed-stop-the-wall-street-recruitment/.

21. Johns Hopkins University Career Center, "Post-Graduate Survey: Class of 2011 Highlights," retrieved from http://www.jhu.edu/careers/Employers/PGShighlightsClassof2011.pdf.

22. The University of Chicago Career Advancement, "Historical Undergraduate Outcomes," retrieved from https://careeradvancement.uchicago.edu/content/outcomes.

23. Georgetown University Cawley Career Education Center, "Senior Survey Outcomes," retrieved from http://careercenter.georgetown.edu/career-exploration/exploring-your-options/senior-survey-outcomes/.

Index

About the Author

Andrew Yang is the founder and CEO of Venture for America, a fellowship program that places top college graduates in startups for two years in emerging US cities (Detroit, New Orleans, Providence, Cincinnati, Las Vegas, Baltimore, Cleveland, Philadelphia, among others) to generate job growth and train the next generation of entrepreneurs. Venture for America is regarded as one of the leading social innovation initiatives in the country today and has a goal of helping create 100,000 new US jobs by 2025. Andrew has worked in startups and early-stage growth companies as a founder or executive for more than twelve years. He was the CEO and president of Manhattan GMAT, a test preparation company that was acquired by the Washington Post Company/Kaplan in 2009. He has also served as the cofounder of an Internet company and an executive at a health care software startup. He has appeared on many media outlets, including CNBC, Fox News, *Time*, Techcrunch, the *Wall Street Journal*, and the *New York Times*, and was named a Champion of Change by the White House for his work with Venture for America as well as one of Fast Company's "100 Most Creative People in Business." He is a graduate of Columbia Law School and Brown University.